H. W. Poff

June 3rd 1864

THE DOCTRINES

AND

DISCIPLINE

OF THE

METHODIST EPISCOPAL CHURCH.

1860.

WITH AN APPENDIX.

New York:
PUBLISHED BY CARLTON & PORTER,
200 MULBERRY-STREET.
1860.

Entered according to Act of Congress, in the year 1860,

BY CARLTON & PORTER,

in the Clerk's Office of the District Court of the United States for the Southern District of New York.

TO THE MEMBERS

OF THE

METHODIST EPISCOPAL CHURCH.

DEARLY BELOVED BRETHREN,—We think it expedient to give you a brief account of the rise of Methodism, both in Europe and America. "In 1729, two young men in England, reading the Bible, saw they could not be saved without holiness: followed after it, and incited others so to do. In 1737, they saw, likewise, that men are justified before they are sanctified: but still holiness was their object. God then thrust them out to raise a holy people."*

In the year 1766, Philip Embury, a

* These are the words of Messrs. Wesley themselves.

Local Preacher of our society, from Ireland, began to preach in the city of New York, and formed a society of his own countrymen and the citizens; and the same year, Thomas Webb preached in a hired room near the barracks. About the same time, Robert Strawbridge, a Local Preacher from Ireland, settled in Frederic County, in the State of Maryland, and, preaching there, formed some societies. The first Methodist Church was built in New York in 1768 or 1769; and in 1769 Richard Boardman and Joseph Pilmoor came to New York, who were the first regular Methodist Preachers on the continent. In the latter end of the year 1771 Francis Asbury and Richard Wright of the same order came over.

We believe that God's design in raising up the Preachers called Methodists in America, was to reform the continent and spread Scripture holiness over these lands. As a proof hereof we have seen since that time a great and glorious work of God from New York through New Jersey, Pennsylvania, Delaware, Maryland, Virginia, North and South Carolina, and Georgia, as also of late to the extremities of the Western and Eastern States.

We esteem it our duty and privilege most earnestly to recommend to *you*, as members of our Church, our FORM OF DISCIPLINE, which has been founded on the experience of a long series of years, as also on the observations and remarks we have made on ancient and modern Churches.

We wish to see this little publication in the house of every Methodist, and the more so as it contains the articles of religion, maintained more or less, in part or in whole, by every reformed Church in the world.

Far from wishing you to be ignorant of any of our doctrines, or any part of our Discipline, we desire you to read, mark, learn, and inwardly digest the whole. You ought, next to the word of God, to procure the articles and canons of the Church to which you belong. This present edition is small and cheap, and we can assure you that the profits of the sale of it shall be applied to charitable and religious purposes.

We remain your very affectionate brethren and pastors, who labor night and day, both in public and in private, for your good.

THOMAS A. MORRIS,
EDMUND S. JANES,
LEVI SCOTT,
MATTHEW SIMPSON,
OSMON C. BAKER,
EDWARD R. AMES.

CONTENTS.

PART II.

THE GOVERNMENT OF THE CHURCH.

CHAPTER I.

THE CONFERENCES.

CHAPTER II.

THE MINISTRY.

CHAPTER III.

BISHOPS.

CHAPTER IV.

PRESIDING ELDERS.

CHAPTER V.

TRAVELING ELDERS.

CHAPTER VI.

TRAVELING DEACONS.

CHAPTER VII.

SUPERANNUATED OR WORN-OUT PREACHERS.

CHAPTER VIII.

LOCAL PREACHERS.

CHAPTER IX.

OF STEWARDS.

CHAPTER X.

THE MEMBERSHIP OF THE CHURCH.

PART III.

THE RITUAL.

PART IV.

BENEVOLENT INSTITUTIONS.

PART V.

TEMPORAL ECONOMY.

CHAPTER I.

RAISING SUPPLIES—CHURCH BUILDINGS, ETC.

CHAPTER II.

BOUNDARIES.

PART VI.

APPENDIX.

THE

DISCIPLINE.

HISTORY OF THE ORIGIN OF THE METHODIST EPISCOPAL CHURCH.

THE preachers and members of our society in general, being convinced that there was a great deficiency of vital religion in the Church of England in America, and being in many places destitute of the Christian Sacraments, as several of the clergy had forsaken their Churches, requested the late Rev. *John Wesley* to take such measures, in his wisdom and prudence, as would afford them suitable relief in their distress.

In consequence of this, our venerable friend, who, under God, had been the father of the great revival of religion now extending over the earth, by the means of the Methodists, determined to ordain ministers for America; and for this purpose, in the year 1784, sent over three regularly ordained clergy: but preferring the episcopal mode of Church government to any other, he solemnly set apart, by the imposition of his hands and prayer, one of them, namely, *Thomas Coke*, Doctor of Civil Law, late of Jesus College, in the University of Oxford, and a presbyter of the Church of England, for the episcopal office; and having delivered to him letters of episcopal orders, commissioned and directed him to set apart *Francis Asbury*, then general assistant of the Methodist Society in America, for the same episcopal office; he, the said *Francis Asbury*, being first ordained deacon and elder. In consequence of which, the said *Francis Asbury* was solemnly set apart for the said episcopal office by prayer, and the imposition of the hands of the said *Thomas Coke*, other regularly ordained ministers assisting in the sacred ceremony. At which time the General Conference, held at Baltimore, did unanimously receive the said *Thomas Coke* and *Francis Asbury* as their bishops, being fully satisfied of the validity of their episcopal ordination.

PART I.

DOCTRINES, ADMINISTRATIVE RULES, AND MEANS OF GRACE.

CHAPTER I.

DOCTRINES AND ORDER OF THE CHURCH.

SECTION I.

Articles of Religion.

I. *Of Faith in the Holy Trinity.*

There is but one living and true God, everlasting, without body or parts, of infinite power, wisdom, and goodness: the maker and preserver of all things, visible and invisible. And in unity of this Godhead, there are three persons, of one substance, power, and eternity, the Father, the Son, and the Holy Ghost.

II. *Of the Word, or Son of God, who was made very Man.*

The Son, who is the Word of the Father, the very and eternal God, of one substance with the Father, took man's nature in the womb of the blessed virgin; so that two whole and perfect natures, that is to say, the Godhead and manhood, were joined together in one person, never to be divided, whereof is one Christ, very God and very man, who truly suffered, was crucified, dead and buried, to reconcile his Father to us, and to be a sacrifice, not only for original guilt, but also for actual sins of men.

III. *Of the Resurrection of Christ.*

Christ did truly rise again from the dead, and took again his body, with all things appertaining to the perfection of man's nature, wherewith he ascended into heaven, and there sitteth until he return to judge all men at the last day.

IV. *Of the Holy Ghost.*

The Holy Ghost, proceeding from the Father and the Son, is of one substance, majesty, and glory with the Father and the Son, very and eternal God.

V. *The Sufficiency of the Holy Scriptures for Salvation.*

The Holy Scriptures contain all things

necessary to salvation; so that whatsoever is not read therein, nor may be proved thereby, is not to be required of any man, that it should be believed as an article of faith, or be thought requisite or necessary to salvation. In the name of the Holy Scripture, we do understand those canonical books of the Old and New Testament, of whose authority was never any doubt in the Church.

The Names of the Canonical Books.

Genesis,
Exodus,
Leviticus,
Numbers,
Deuteronomy,
Joshua,
Judges,
Ruth,
The First Book of Samuel,
The Second Book of Samuel,
The First Book of Kings,
The Second Book of Kings,
The First Book of Chronicles,
The Second Book of Chronicles,
The Book of Ezra,
The Book of Nehemiah,
The Book of Esther,

The Book of Job,
The Psalms,
The Proverbs,
Ecclesiastes, or the Preacher,
Cantica, or Songs of Solomon,
Four Prophets the greater,
Twelve Prophets the less:

All the books of the New Testament, as they are commonly received, we do receive and account canonical.

VI. *Of the Old Testament.*

The Old Testament is not contrary to the New; for both in the Old and New Testament everlasting life is offered to mankind by Christ, who is the only Mediator between God and man, being both God and man. Wherefore they are not to be heard who feign that the old fathers did look only for transitory promises. Although the law given from God by Moses, as touching ceremonies and rites, doth not bind Christians, nor ought the civil precepts thereof of necessity be received in any commonwealth; yet, notwithstanding, no Christian whatsoever is free from the obedience of the commandments which are called moral.

VII. *Of Original or Birth Sin.*

Original sin standeth not in the following of Adam, (as the Pelagians do vainly talk,) but it is the corruption of the nature of every man, that naturally is engendered of the offspring of Adam, whereby man is very far gone from original righteousness, and of his own nature inclined to evil, and that continually.

VIII. *Of Free Will.*

The condition of man after the fall of Adam is such, that he cannot turn and prepare himself, by his own natural strength and works, to faith, and calling upon God; wherefore we have no power to do good works, pleasant and acceptable to God, without the grace of God by Christ preventing us, that we may have a good will, and working with us, when we have that good will.

IX. *Of the Justification of Man.*

We are accounted righteous before God, only for the merit of our Lord and Saviour Jesus Christ by faith, and not for our own works or deservings. Wherefore, that we are justified by faith only, is a most wholesome doctrine, and very full of comfort.

X. *Of Good Works.*

Although good works, which are the fruits of faith, and follow after justification, cannot put away our sins, and endure the severity of God's judgments; yet are they pleasing and acceptable to God in Christ, and spring out of a true and lively faith, insomuch that by them a lively faith may be as evidently known as a tree is discerned by its fruit.

XI. *Of Works of Supererogation.*

Voluntary works, besides, over, and above God's commandments, which are called works of supererogation, cannot be taught without arrogancy and impiety. For by them men do declare that they do not only render unto God as much as they are bound to do, but that they do more for his sake than of bounden duty is required: whereas Christ saith plainly, When ye have done all that is commanded you, say, We are unprofitable servants.

XII. *Of Sin after Justification.*

Not every sin willingly committed after justification is the sin against the Holy Ghost, and unpardonable. Wherefore, the grant of repentance is not to be denied to such as fall into sin after justification: after we have received the Holy Ghost, we may depart from grace given, and fall into sin, and, by the grace of God, rise again and amend our lives. And therefore they are to be condemned who say they can no more sin as long as they live here; or deny the place of forgiveness to such as truly repent.

XIII. *Of the Church.*

The visible Church of Christ is a congregation of faithful men, in which the pure word of God is preached, and the sacraments duly administered, according to Christ's ordinance, in all those things that of necessity are requisite to the same.

XIV. *Of Purgatory.*

The Romish doctrine concerning purgatory, pardon, worshiping, and adoration, as well of images as of relics, and also invocation of saints, is a fond thing, vainly invented, and grounded upon no warrant of Scripture, but repugnant to the word of God.

XV. *Of speaking in the Congregation in such a Tongue as the People understand.*

It is a thing plainly repugnant to the word of God, and the custom of the primitive Church, to have public prayer in the Church, or to minister the sacraments, in a tongue not understood by the people.

XVI. *Of the Sacraments.*

Sacraments, ordained of Christ, are not only badges or tokens of Christian men's profession; but rather they are certain signs of grace, and God's good will toward us, by the which he doth work invisibly in us, and doth not only quicken, but also strengthen and confirm our faith in him.

There are two sacraments ordained of Christ our Lord in the Gospel; that is to say, Baptism and the Supper of the Lord.

Those five commonly called sacraments, that is to say, confirmation, penance, orders, matrimony, and extreme unction, are not to be counted for sacraments of the Gospel, being such as have partly grown out of the *corrupt* following of the apostles; and partly are states of life allowed in the Scriptures, but yet have not the like nature of Baptism and the Lord's Supper, because they have not any visible sign or ceremony ordained of God.

The sacraments were not ordained of Christ to be gazed upon, or to be carried about; but that we should duly use them.

And in such only as worthily receive the same, they have a wholesome effect or operation: but they that receive them unworthily, purchase to themselves condemnation, as St. Paul saith. 1 Cor. xi, 29.

XVII. *Of Baptism.*

Baptism is not only a sign of profession, and mark of difference, whereby Christians are distinguished from others that are not baptized; but it is also a sign of regeneration, or the new birth. The baptism of young children is to be retained in the Church.

XVIII. *Of the Lord's Supper.*

The Supper of the Lord is not only a sign of the love that Christians ought to have among themselves one to another, but rather is a sacrament of our redemption by Christ's death; insomuch that, to such as rightly, worthily, and with faith receive the same, the bread which we break is a partaking of the body of Christ; and likewise the cup of blessing is a partaking of the blood of Christ.

Transubstantiation, or the change of the substance of bread and wine in the Supper of our Lord, cannot be proved by Holy Writ, but is repugnant to the plain words of Scripture, overthroweth the nature of a sacrament, and hath given occasion to many superstitions.

The body of Christ is given, taken, and eaten in the Supper, only after a heavenly and spiritual manner. And the means whereby the body of Christ is received and eaten in the Supper, is faith.

The sacrament of the Lord's Supper was not by Christ's ordinance reserved, carried about, lifted up, or worshiped.

XIX. *Of both Kinds.*

The cup of the Lord is not to be denied to the lay people; for both the parts of the Lord's Supper, by Christ's ordinance and commandment, ought to be administered to all Christians alike.

XX. *Of the one Oblation of Christ, finished upon the Cross.*

The offering of Christ, once made, is that perfect redemption, propitiation, and satisfaction for all the sins of the whole world, both original and actual; and there is none other satisfaction for sin but that alone. Wherefore the sacrifice of masses, in the which it is commonly said that the priest doth offer Christ for the quick and the dead, to have remission of pain or guilt, is a blasphemous fable, and dangerous deceit.

XXI. *Of the Marriage of Ministers.*

The ministers of Christ are not commanded by God's law either to vow the estate of single life, or to abstain from marriage: therefore it is lawful for them, as for all other Christians, to marry at their own discretion, as they shall judge the same to serve best to godliness.

XXII. *Of the Rites and Ceremonies of Churches.*

It is not necessary that rites and ceremonies should in all places be the same, or exactly alike; for they have been always different, and may be changed according to the diversity of countries, times, and men's manners, so that nothing be ordained against God's word. Whosoever, through his private judgment, willingly and purposely doth openly break the rites and ceremonies of the Church to which he belongs, which are not repugnant to the word of God, and are ordained and approved by common authority, ought to be rebuked openly, that others may fear to do the like, as one that offendeth against the common order of the Church, and woundeth the consciences of weak brethren.

Every particular Church may ordain, change, or abolish rites and ceremonies, so that all things may be done to edification.

XXIII. *Of the Rulers of the United States of America.*

The president, the congress, the general assemblies, the governors, and the councils of state, *as the delegates of the people*, are the rulers of the United States of America, according to the division of power made to them by the Constitution of the United States, and by the constitutions of their respective states. And the said states are a sovereign and independent nation, and ought not to be subject to any foreign jurisdiction.*

* As far as it respects civil affairs, we believe it the duty of Christians, and especially all Christian ministers, to be subject to the supreme authority of the country where they may reside, and to use all laudable means to enjoin obedience to the powers that be; and therefore it is expected that all our preachers and people, who may be under the British or any other government, will behave themselves as peaceable and orderly subjects.

XXIV. *Of Christian Men's Goods.*

The riches and goods of Christians are not common, as touching the right, title, and possession of the same, as some do falsely boast. Notwithstanding, every man ought, of such things as he possesseth, liberally to give alms to the poor, according to his ability.

XXV. *Of a Christian Man's Oath.*

As we confess that vain and rash swearing is forbidden Christian men by our Lord Jesus Christ and James his apostle; so we judge that the Christian religion doth not prohibit, but that a man may swear when the magistrate requireth, in a cause of faith and charity, so it be done according to the prophet's teaching, in justice, judgment, and truth.

SECTION II.

The General Rules.

THE NATURE, DESIGN, AND GENERAL RULES OF OUR UNITED SOCIETIES.

(1) IN the latter end of the year 1739, eight or ten persons came to Mr. Wesley in London, who appeared to be deeply con-

vinced of sin, and earnestly groaning for redemption. They desired (as did two or three more the next day) that he would spend some time with them in prayer, and advise them how to flee from the wrath to come; which they saw continually hanging over their heads. That he might have more time for this great work, he appointed a day when they might all come together; which from thenceforward they did every week, namely, on *Thursday*, in the evening. To these, and as many more as desired to join with them, (for their number increased daily,) he gave those advices from time to time which he judged most needful for them; and they always concluded their meeting with prayer suited to their several necessities.

(2) This was the rise of the UNITED SOCIETY, first in *Europe*, and then in *America*. Such a society is no other than "*a company of men* having the form and seeking the power of *godliness, united in order to pray together, to receive the word of exhortation, and to watch over one another in love, that they may help each other to work out their salvation.*"

(3) That it may the more easily be discerned whether they are indeed working

out their own salvation, each society is divided into smaller companies, called classes, according to their respective places of abode. There are about twelve persons in a class; one of whom is styled *the leader*. It is his duty,

I. To see each person in his class once a week at least; in order,

1. To inquire how their souls prosper.

2. To advise, reprove, comfort, or exhort as occasion may require.

3. To receive what they are willing to give toward the relief of the preachers, Church, and poor.*

II. To meet the ministers and the stewards of the society once a week; in order,

1. To inform the minister of any that are sick, or of any that walk disorderly, and will not be reproved.

2. To pay the stewards what they have received of their several classes in the week preceding.

(4) There is only one condition previously required of those who desire admission into these societies, "a desire to flee from the wrath to come, and to be saved from

* This part refers to towns and cities; where the poor are generally numerous, and Church expenses considerable.

their sins." But wherever this is really fixed in the soul, it will be shown by its fruits. It is therefore expected of all who continue therein, that they should continue to evidence their desire of salvation,

First, By doing no harm, by avoiding evil of every kind, especially that which is most generally practiced; such as,

The taking of the name of God in vain.

The profaning the day of the Lord, either by doing ordinary work therein, or by buying or selling.

Drunkenness, buying or selling spirituous liquors, or drinking them, unless in cases of extreme necessity.

The buying and selling of men, women, and children, with an intention to enslave them.

Fighting, quarreling, brawling, brother *going to law* with brother; returning evil for evil; or railing for railing; the *using many words* in buying or selling.

The *buying or selling goods that have not paid the duty.*

The *giving or taking things on usury*, that is, unlawful interest.

Uncharitable or *unprofitable* conversation; particularly speaking evil of magistrates or of ministers.

Doing to others as we would not they should do unto us.

Doing what we know is not for the glory of God; as,

The *putting on of gold and costly apparel.*

The *taking such diversions* as cannot be used in the name of the Lord Jesus.

The *singing* those *songs*, or *reading* those *books*, which do not tend to the knowledge or love of God.

Softness and needless self-indulgence.

Laying up treasure upon earth.

Borrowing without a probability of paying; or taking up goods without a probability of paying for them.

(5) It is expected of all who continue in these societies, that they should continue to evidence their desire of salvation,

Secondly, By doing good; by being in every kind merciful after their power; as they have opportunity, doing good of every possible sort, and, as far as possible, to all men.

To their bodies, of the ability which God giveth, by giving food to the hungry, by clothing the naked, by visiting or helping them that are sick or in prison.

To their souls, by instructing, reproving,

or exhorting all we have any intercourse with; trampling under foot that enthusiastic doctrine, that "we are not to do good unless *our hearts be free to it.*"

By doing good, especially to them that are of the household of faith, or groaning so to be; employing them preferably to others; buying one of another; helping each other in business; and so much the more because the world will love its own, and them *only.*

By all possible *diligence* and *frugality*, that the Gospel be not blamed.

By running with patience the race which is set before them, *denying themselves, and taking up their cross daily;* submitting to bear the reproach of Christ, to be as the filth and offscouring of the world; and looking that men should say *all manner of evil of them falsely for the Lord's sake.*

(6) It is expected of all who desire to continue in these societies, that they should continue to evidence their desire of salvation,

Thirdly, By attending upon all the ordinances of God: such are,

The public worship of God:

The ministry of the word, either read or expounded:

The Supper of the Lord:
Family and private prayer:
Searching the Scriptures; and
Fasting or abstinence.

(7) These are the general rules of our societies: all which we are taught of God to observe, even in his written word, which is the only rule, and the sufficient rule, both of our faith and practice. And all these we know his Spirit writes on truly awakened hearts. If there be any among us who observe them not, who habitually break any of them, let it be known unto them who watch over that soul as they who must give an account. We will admonish him of the error of his ways. We will bear with him for a season. But if then he repent not, he hath no more place among us. We have delivered our own souls.

SECTION III.

The Relation of Baptized Children to the Church.

Quest. 1. Are all young children entitled to baptism?

Answ. We hold that all children, by virtue of the unconditional benefits of the atonement, are members of the kingdom of God, and, therefore, graciously entitled to baptism; but as infant baptism contemplates a course of religious instruction and discipline, it is expected of all parents or guardians who present their children for baptism, that they use all diligence in bringing them up in conformity to the word of God, and they should be solemnly admonished of this obligation, and earnestly exhorted to faithfulness therein.

Quest. 2. What is the relation of baptized children to the Church?

Answ. We regard all children who have been baptized, as placed in visible covenant relation to God, and under the special care and supervision of the Church.

Quest. 3. What shall be done for the baptized children of our Church?

Answ. 1. The preacher in charge shall preserve a full and accurate register of the names of all the baptized children within his pastoral care; the dates of their birth, baptism, their parentage, and places of residence.

Answ. 2. As early as they shall be able to understand, let them be taught the nature, design, and obligations of their baptism, and the truths of religion necessary to make them wise unto salvation; let them be encouraged to attend class, and to give regular attendance upon all the means of grace, according to their age, capacity, and religious experience.

Answ. 3. Whenever they shall have attained an age sufficient to understand the obligations of religion, and shall give evidence of a desire to flee from the wrath to come, and to be saved from their sins, their names shall be enrolled in the list of probationers; and if they shall continue to give evidence of a principle and habit of piety, they may be admitted into full membership in our Church, on the recommendation of a leader with whom they have met at least six months in class, by publicly assenting before the Church to the baptismal covenant, and also the usual questions on doctrines and discipline.

Answ. 4. Whenever a baptized child shall by orphanage, or otherwise, become deprived of Christian guardianship, th preacher in charge shall ascertain and report to the Leaders' Meeting the facts in the case; and such provision shall be made for the Christian training of the child, as the circumstances of the case admit and require.

SECTION IV.

Rules concerning Dress.

Quest. Should we insist on the rules concerning dress?

Answ. By all means. This is no time to encourage superfluity in dress. Therefore, let all our people be exhorted to conform to the spirit of the apostolic precept, not to adorn themselves "with gold, or pearls, or costly array." 1 Tim. ii, 9.

SECTION V.

Rules relating to Marriage.

Quest. 1. Do we observe any evil which has prevailed in our Church with respect to marriage?

Answ. Many of our members have married with *unawakened* persons. This has produced bad effects; they have been either hindered for life, or have turned back to perdition.

Quest. 2. What can be done to discourage this?

Answ. 1. Let every preacher publicly enforce the apostle's caution, "Be ye not unequally yoked together with unbelievers." 2 Cor. vi, 14.

2. Let all be exhorted to take no step in so weighty a matter, without advising with the most serious of their brethren.

Quest. 3. Ought any woman to marry without the consent of her parents?

Answ. In general she ought not. Yet there may be exceptions. For if, 1. A woman believe it to be her duty to marry: if, 2. Her parents absolutely refuse to let her marry any Christian: then she may, nay, ought to marry without their consent. Yet even then a Methodist preacher ought not to be married to her.

We do not prohibit our people from marrying persons who are not of our Church, provided such persons have the form, and are seeking the power of godliness; but we are determined to discourage their marrying persons who do not come up to this description.

CHAPTER II.

MEANS OF GRACE.

SECTION I.

Public Worship.

Quest. 1. WHAT directions shall be given for the establishment of uniformity in public worship among us on the Lord's day?

Answ. 1. Let the morning service consist of singing, prayer, the reading of a chapter out of the Old Testament, and another out of the New, and preaching.

2. Let the afternoon service consist of singing, prayer, the reading of one or two chapters out of the Bible, and preaching.

3. Let the evening service consist of singing, prayer, and preaching.

4. But on the days of administering the Lord's Supper, the two chapters in the morning service may be omitted.

5. In administering the ordinances, and in the burial of the dead, let the form of Discipline invariably be used. Let the Lord's Prayer also be used on all occasions of public worship in concluding the first

prayer, and the apostolic benediction in dismissing the congregation.

6. Let the Society be met, wherever it is practicable, on the Sabbath-day.

Quest. 2. Is there not a great indecency sometimes practiced among us, namely, talking in the congregation before and after service? How shall this be cured?

Answ. Let all the Ministers and Preachers join as one man, and enlarge on the impropriety of talking before or after service; and strongly exhort those that are concerned to do it no more. In three months, if we are in earnest, this vile practice will be banished out of every Methodist congregation. Let none stop till he has carried his point.

SECTION II.

The Spirit and Truth of Singing.

Quest. How shall we guard against formality in singing?

Answ. 1. Choose such hymns as are proper for the occasion, and do not sing too much at once; seldom more than four or five verses.

2. Let the tune be suited to the sentiment, and do not suffer the people to sing too slow.

3. In every Society let due attention be given to the cultivation of sacred music.

4. If you cannot sing yourself, let one or two be chosen in each Society to lead the singing.

5. As singing is a part of Divine worship in which all ought to unite, therefore exhort every person in the congregation to sing, not one in ten only.

SECTION III.

Class-meetings and Love-feasts.

Quest. 1. How may the Leaders of classes be rendered more useful?

Answ. 1. Let each of them be diligently examined concerning his method of meeting a class. Let this be done with all possible exactness, at least once a quarter. In order to this, take sufficient time.

2. Let each Leader carefully inquire how every soul of his class prospers: not only how each person observes the outward rules, but how he grows in the knowledge and love of God.

3. Let the Leaders converse with those who have the charge of their circuits, frequently and freely.

Quest. 2. Can anything more be done in order to make the Class-meetings lively and profitable?

Ans. 1. Change improper Leaders.

2. Let the Leaders frequently meet each other's classes.

3. Let us observe which Leaders are the most useful; and let these meet the other classes as often as possible.

4. See that all the Leaders be not only men of sound judgment, but men truly devoted to God.

Quest. 3. What shall we do with those members of our Church who willfully and repeatedly neglect to meet their class?

Answ. 1. Let the Elder, Deacon, or one of the Preachers visit them, whenever it is practicable, and explain to them the consequence if they continue to neglect, namely, exclusion.

2. If they do not amend, let him who has the charge of the circuit or station bring their case before the Society, or a select number, before whom they shall have been cited to appear; and if they be found guilty of willful neglect by a decision of a majority of the members before whom their case is brought, let them be laid aside, and let the Preacher show that they

are excluded for a breach of our rules, and not for immoral conduct.

Quest. 4. How often shall we permit serious persons who are not of our Church to meet in class?

Answ. At every other meeting of the class in every place let no stranger be admitted. At other times they may; but the same person not above twice or thrice.

Quest. 5. How often shall we permit strangers to be present at our Love-feasts?

Answ. Let them be admitted with the utmost caution; and the same person on no account above twice or thrice, unless he become a member.

PART II.

THE GOVERNMENT OF THE CHURCH.

CHAPTER I.

THE CONFERENCES.

SECTION I.

Of our Deportment at the Conferences.

IT is desired that all things be considered on these occasions as in the immediate presence of God; that every person speak freely whatever is in his heart.

Quest. How may we best improve our time at the conferences?

Answ. 1. While we are conversing, let us have an especial care to set God always before us.

2. In the intermediate hours, let us redeem all the time we can for private exercises.

3. Therein let us give ourselves to prayer for one another, and for a blessing on our labor.

SECTION II.

The General Conference.

Quest. Who shall compose the General Conference, and what are the regulations and powers belonging to it?

Answ. 1. The General Conference shall be composed of one member for every thirty members of each Annual Conference, to be appointed either by seniority or choice, at the discretion of such Annual Conference; yet so that such representatives shall have traveled at least four full calendar years from the time that they were received on trial by an Annual Conference, and are in full connection at the time of holding the Conference.

2. The General Conference shall meet on the first day of May, in the year of our Lord 1812, in the city of New York, and thenceforward on the first day of May once in four years perpetually, in such place or places as shall be fixed on by the General Conference from time to time; but the general superintendents, or a majority of them, by or with the advice of two thirds of all the Annual Conferences, or, if there be no general superintendent, two thirds of all the Annual Conferences, shall have

power to call an extra session of the General Conference at any time, to be constituted in the usual way.

3. At all times when the General Conference is met, it shall take two thirds of the representatives of all the Annual Conferences to make a quorum for transacting business.

4. One of the general superintendents shall preside in the General Conference; but in case no general superintendent be present, the General Conference shall choose a president *pro tem.*

5. The General Conference may try appeals from members of Annual Conferences who may have been censured, suspended, expelled, or located without their consent, by a committee embracing not less than fifteen of its members, nor more than one member from each delegation, who, in the presence of a Bishop presiding, and one or more of the Secretaries of the Conference keeping a faithful record of all the proceedings had, shall have full power to hear and determine the case, subject to the rules and regulations which govern the said Conference in such proceedings, and the records made and the papers submitted in such trials shall be presented to the Con-

ference, and be filed and preserved with the papers of that body.

6. The General Conference shall have full powers to make rules and regulations for our Church, under the following limitations and restrictions, namely:

1. The General Conference shall not revoke, alter, or change our Articles of Religion, nor establish any new standards or rules of doctrine contrary to our present existing and established standards of doctrine.
2. They shall not allow of more than one representative for every fourteen members of the Annual Conference, nor allow of a less number than one for every forty-five; provided, nevertheless, that when there shall be in any Annual Conference a fraction of two thirds the number which shall be fixed for the ratio of representation, such Annual Conference shall be entitled to an additional delegate for such fraction; and provided, also, that no Conference shall be denied the privilege of two delegates.
3. They shall not change or alter any part or rule of our government, so as to do away episcopacy, or destroy the plan of our itinerant general superintendency.

4. They shall not revoke or change the General Rules of the United Societies.
5. They shall not do away the privileges of our ministers or preachers of trial by a committee, and of an appeal; neither shall they do away the privileges of our members of trial before the society, or by a committee, and of an appeal.
6. They shall not appropriate the produce of the Book Concern, nor of the Charter Fund, to any purpose other than for the benefit of the traveling, supernumerary, superannuated, and worn-out preachers, their wives, widows, and children. *Provided*, nevertheless, that upon the concurrent recommendation of three fourths of all the members of the several Annual Conferences, who shall be present and vote on such recommendation, then a majority of two thirds of the General Conference succeeding shall suffice to alter any of the above restrictions, excepting the first article: and also, whenever such alteration or alterations shall have been first recommended by two thirds of the General Conference, so soon as three fourths of the members of all the Annual Conferences shall have concurred as aforesaid, such alteration or alterations shall take effect.

To defray the expenses of the delegates composing the General Conference, a collection shall be taken up in each circuit and station some time previously to the sitting of the Conference, and the sums so collected shall be brought up by the delegation to the General Conference, and applied to the object herein contemplated, in proportion to the expenses of the several delegates.

SECTION III.

The Annual Conference.

Quest. 1. Who shall attend the Annual Conferences?

Answ. All the Traveling Preachers—both those who are in full connection, and those who are on trial.

Quest. 2. Who shall appoint the times of holding the Annual Conferences?

Answ. The Bishops: but they shall allow the Annual Conferences to sit a week at least.

Quest. 3. Who shall appoint the places of holding the Annual Conferences?

Answ. Each Annual Conference shall appoint the place of its own sitting; but, should it become necessary, from any unforeseen cause, to change the place of its sitting after it has been fixed by the Conference, the Preacher or Preachers in charge of the place, and the Presiding Elder of the district where the Conference was to be held, shall have power to make such change. But this authority shall not be exercised without first consulting the other Presiding Elders of the Conference so far as practicable.

Quest. 4. Who shall preside at the Annual Conferences?

Answ. The Bishop. In case no Bishop be present, a Presiding Elder, appointed by a Bishop, by letter or otherwise, shall preside. But if no appointment be made, or if the Presiding Elder appointed do not attend, the Conference shall in either of these cases elect the President by ballot, without a debate, from among the Presiding Elders.

Quest. 5. What is the method wherein we usually proceed in the Annual Conferences?

Answ. We inquire,

1. What Preachers are admitted on trial?
2. Who remain on trial?
3. Who are admitted into full connection?
4. Who are the Deacons?
5. Who have been elected and ordained Elders this year?

6. Who have located this year?
7. Who are the superannuated or worn-out Preachers?
8. Who have been expelled from the connection this year?
9. Who have withdrawn from the connection this year?
10. Are all the Preachers blameless in life and conversation?
11. Who have died this year?
12. What is the number of Church members?
 Number of deaths the past year?
 Number of probationers?
 Number of Local Preachers?
 Number of adults baptized the past year?
 Number of children baptized the past year?
 Number of churches?
 Their probable value?
 Number of parsonages?
 Their probable value?
 Amount collected for Superannuated Preachers?
 Amount collected for the Missionary Society?
 Amount collected for the Tract Society?
 Amount collected for the American Bible Society?

Amount collected for the Sunday-School Union?
Number of Sunday-schools?
Number of officers and teachers?
Number of scholars?
Number of volumes in library?

13. What amounts are necessary for the Superannuated Preachers, and the widows and orphans of Preachers, and to make up the deficiencies of those who have not obtained their regular allowance on the circuits?
14. What has been collected on the foregoing accounts, and how has it been applied?
15. Where are the Preachers stationed this year?
16. Where and when shall our next Conference be held?

Quest. 6. Is there any other business to be done in the Annual Conferences?

Answ. 1. The electing and ordaining of Deacons and Elders.

2. It shall be the duty of each Annual Conference to examine strictly into the state of the domestic missions within its bounds, and to allow none to remain on the list of its missions which, in the judgment of the Conference, is able to support itself.

Quest. 7. Are there any other directions

to be given concerning the Annual Conferences?

Answ. 1. There shall be fifty-one Conferences in the year.

2. A record of the proceedings of each Annual Conference shall be kept by a Secretary, chosen for the purpose, and shall be signed by the President and Secretary; and let a copy of said record be sent to the General Conference.*

3. Every Annual Conference has full liberty to adopt and recommend such plans and rules as to them may appear necessary the more effectually to raise supplies for the respective allowances. Each Annual Conference is authorized to raise a fund, if they judge it proper, subject to its own control, and under such regulations as their wisdom may direct, for the relief of the distressed traveling and superannuated preachers, their wives, widows, and children; and it shall be the duty of each Annual Conference to take measures *from year to year* to raise money in every circuit and station within its bounds for those purposes.

4. Each Annual Conference shall report through its Secretary to the Sunday-School

* For duties of Secretary see Appendix A.

Union the number of schools within its bounds, together with other facts named in the form published by the Union, and contained in the annual reports of preachers, as directed in part ii, chapter ii, section 12, answer 19 to question 1, page 87.

[N. B.—For duty of an Annual Conference to Estimate for Bishop, etc., see p. 96.]

SECTION IV.

The Quarterly Conference.

Quest. 1. Of whom shall the Quarterly Conferences be composed?

Answ. Of all the Traveling and Local Preachers, exhorters, stewards, and class-leaders of the circuit or station, and the first male superintendents of our Sunday-Schools, being members of our Church, and approved by the Quarterly Conference, and none else. The Missionary Committee shall have a right to a seat during the action of the Conference on the subject of Missions, but at no other time.

Quest. 2. Who shall preside in the Quarterly Conferences?

Answ. The Presiding Elder, and in his absence the Preacher in charge.

Quest. 3. How shall the minutes of the Quarterly Conference be kept?

Answ. The Quarterly Conference shall appoint a Secretary to take down the proceedings thereof, in a book kept by one of the stewards of the circuit for that purpose.

Quest. 4. What shall be the regular business of the Quarterly Conference?

Answ. 1. To hear complaints, and to receive and try appeals.

2. To take cognizance of all the Local Preachers in the circuit or station, and to inquire into the gifts, labors, and usefulness of each Preacher by name; to license proper persons to preach, and renew their license annually, when, in the judgment of said Conference, their gifts, grace, and usefulness will warrant such renewal; to recommend to the Annual Conference suitable candidates in the local connection for Deacons' or Elders' orders, and for admission on trial in the traveling connection; and to try, suspend, expel, or acquit any Local Preacher in the circuit or station against whom charges may be brought. *Provided*, that no person shall be licensed to preach without the recommendation of the society of which he is a member, or of a Leaders' Meeting; nor shall any one be licensed to preach, or recommended to

the Annual Conference to travel, or for ordination, without first being examined in the Quarterly Conference on the subject of doctrines and discipline.

3. To appoint Stewards, the Preacher in charge having a right to nominate; and to examine the characters of exhorters annually, and recommend them, if approved, for renewal of license.

4. To appoint District Stewards as provided for in part ii, chap. ix, and a Parsonage Committee, if necessary.*

5. To appoint a Missionary Committee, as provided for in part iv, § 2, item 4.

6. To receive the annual reports of Trustees, as provided for in part v, ch. 1, § 4, item 6.

7. Each Quarterly Conference shall have supervision of all the Sunday-schools and Sunday-school Societies within its bounds, which schools and societies shall be auxiliary to the Sunday-School Union of the Methodist Episcopal Church.

8. It shall be the duty of the Quarterly Conference of each Circuit and Station, at the session immediately preceding the Annual Conference, to appoint an Estimating Committee, consisting of three or more

* See part v, ch. i, § 2.

members of the Church, who shall, after conferring with the preachers, make an estimate of the amount necessary to furnish a comfortable support to the preacher or preachers stationed among them, taking into consideration the number and condition of the family or families of such preacher or preachers, which estimate shall be subject to the action of the Quarterly Conference, and the stewards shall provide by such methods as they may judge best to meet such amount. The traveling and moving expenses of the preachers shall not be reckoned as a part of the estimate, but be paid by the Stewards separately.

9. It shall be the duty of the Quarterly Conference of each charge within whose bounds a superannuated preacher, or the widow or child of a deceased preacher may reside, to appoint a committee, whose duty it shall be to make an estimate of the amount necessary to assist such preacher, widow, or child in obtaining a comfortable support, and such estimate shall be sent up to the Annual Conference with which the claimant may be connected, and subject to the action of said Annual Conference.

Quest. 5. What is the method wherein

we usually proceed in the Quarterly Conferences?

Answ. We inquire:

1. Are there any complaints?

2. Are there any appeals?

3. Is there a written report of the number and state of the Sabbath-schools, and of the religious instruction of the children?

4. Will you have a Sabbath-school Committee?

5. What amount is estimated for the support of the pastor or pastors of this charge the present year?

6. What amount has been received for the support of the pastor or pastors the present quarter?

7. Who constitute the Missionary Committee?

8. Is there any change desired in the Board of Stewards?

9. Are there any further reports (a) from the pastor, (b) from the stewards, (c) from the trustees, (d) from committees?

10. What amounts have been contributed (a) for Missions, (b) for Sunday-School Union, (c) for Tract Cause?

11. How many subscribers have been obtained for our periodicals?

12. Are there any recommendations for license to preach?

13. Are the Church records properly kept?

14. Who constitute the Estimating Committee for the ensuing year?

15. Who is the district steward?

16. Is there any other business?

[In answer to this, at the fourth Quarterly Conference, the examination of local preachers, exhorters, and stewards, and the licensing of local preachers and exhorters, and recommendations to the Annual Conference for orders, or for admission into the traveling connection.]

N. B. 1. On circuits, the Quarterly Conference determines the place of the Quarterly Meeting, and the Presiding Elder fixes the time.

N. B. 2. Questions 10 and 11 are asked only at the fourth Quarterly Conference, and question 4 only at the first Quarterly Conference.

CHAPTER II.

THE MINISTRY.

SECTION 1.

The Examination of those who think they are moved by the Holy Ghost to Preach.

Quest. How shall we try those who profess to be moved by the Holy Ghost to preach?

Ans. 1. Let the following questions be asked, namely: Do they know God as a pardoning God? Have they the love of God abiding in them? Do they desire nothing but God? And are they holy in all manner of conversation?

2. Have they gifts (as well as grace) for the work? Have they (in some tolerable degree) a clear, sound understanding, a right judgment in the things of God, a just conception of salvation by faith? And has God given them any degree of utterance? Do they speak justly, readily, clearly?

3. Have they fruit? Are any truly convinced of sin, and converted to God by their preaching?

As long as these three marks concur in

any one, we believe he is called of God to preach. These we receive as sufficient proof that he is moved by the Holy Ghost

SECTION II.

Rules for a Preacher's Conduct.

Quest. 1. What are the directions given to a Preacher?

Answ. 1. Be diligent. Never be unemployed: never be triflingly employed. Never trifle away time; neither spend any more time at any place than is strictly necessary.

2. Be serious. Let your motto be *Holiness to the Lord.* Avoid all lightness, jesting, and foolish talking.

3. Converse sparingly, and conduct yourself prudently with women. 1 Tim. v, 2.

4. Take no step toward marriage without first consulting with your brethren.

5. Believe evil of no one without good evidence; unless you see it done, take heed how you credit it. Put the best construction on everything. You know the judge is always supposed to be on the prisoner's side.

6. Speak evil of no one; because your word, especially, would eat as doth a canker.

Keep your thoughts within your own breast till you come to the person concerned.

7. Tell every one under your care what you think wrong in his conduct and temper, and that lovingly and plainly as soon as may be: else it will fester in your heart. Make all haste to cast the fire out of your bosom.

8. Avoid all affectation. A preacher of the Gospel is the servant of all.

9. Be ashamed of nothing but sin.

10. Be punctual. Do everything exactly at the time. And do not mend our rules, but keep them; not for wrath, but conscience' sake.

11. You have nothing to do but to save souls: therefore spend and be spent in this work; and go always not only to those that want you, but to those that want you most.

Observe! it is not your business only to preach so many times, and to take care of this or that society, but to save as many as you can; to bring as many sinners as you can to repentance, and with all your power to build them up in that holiness without which they cannot see the Lord. And remember! a Methodist preacher is to mind every point, great and small, in the Methodist Discipline! Therefore you will need to exercise all the sense and grace you have.

12. Act in all things not according to your own will, but as a son in the Gospel. As such, it is your duty to employ your time in the manner in which we direct: in preaching, and visiting from house to house; in reading, meditation, and prayer. Above all, if you labor with us in the Lord's vineyard, it is needful you should do that part of the work which we advise, at those times and places which we judge most for his glory.

Quest. 2. Are there any smaller advices which might be of use to us?

Answ. Perhaps these: 1. Be sure never to disappoint a congregation. 2. Begin at the time appointed. 3. Let your whole deportment be serious, weighty, and solemn. 4. Always suit your subject to your audience. 5. Choose the plainest text you can. 6. Take care not to ramble, but keep to your text, and make out what you take in hand. 7. Take care of anything awkward or affected, either in your gesture, phrase, or pronunciation. 8. Do not usually pray *extempore* above eight or ten minutes (at most) without intermission. 9. Frequently read and enlarge upon a portion of Scripture; and let young preachers often exhort without taking a text. 10. Always avail yourself of the great festivals, by preaching on the occasion.

SECTION III.

The Duty of Preachers to God, themselves, and one another.

Quest. 1. What is the duty of a Preacher?

Answ. 1. To preach.

2. To meet the societies and classes.

3. To visit the sick.

4. To preach in the morning where he can get hearers. We recommend morning preaching at five o'clock in the summer, and six in the winter, wherever it is practicable.

Quest. 2. How shall a Preacher be qualified for his charge?

Answ. By walking closely with God, and having his work greatly at heart; and by understanding and loving discipline, ours in particular.

Quest. 3. Do we sufficiently watch over each other?

Answ. We do not. Should we not frequently ask each other, Do you walk closely with God? Have you now fellowship with the Father and the Son? At what hour do you rise? Do you punctually observe the morning and evening hours of retirement? Do you spend the day in the manner which the Conference advises? Do you converse seriously, usefully, and closely? To be more particular: Do you use all the means of grace yourself, and enforce the use of them on all other persons? They are either instituted or prudential.

I. The instituted are,

1. Prayer: private, family, and public; consisting of deprecation, petition, intercession, and thanksgiving. Do you use each of these? Do you forecast daily, wherever you are, to secure time for private devotion? Do you practice it everywhere? Do you ask everywhere, Have you family prayer? Do you ask individuals, Do you use private prayer, every morning and evening in particular?

2. Searching the Scriptures, by

(1.) Reading: constantly, some part of every day; regularly, all the Bible in order; carefully, with notes; seriously, with prayer before and after; fruitfully, immediately practicing what you learn there?

(2.) Meditating: At set times? By rule?

(3.) Hearing: Every opportunity? With prayer before, at, after? Have you a Bible always about you?

3. The Lord's Supper: Do you use this at every opportunity? With solemn prayer before? With earnest and deliberate self-devotion?

4. Fasting: Do you use as much abstinence and fasting every week as your health, strength, and labor will permit.

5. Christian conference: Are you convinced how important and how difficult it is to order your conversation aright? Is it always in grace? Seasoned with salt? Meet to minister grace to the hearers? Do you not converse too long at a time? Is not an hour commonly enough? Would it not be well always to have a determined end in view? And to pray before and after it?

II. Prudential means we may use either as Christians, as Methodists, or as Preachers.

1. As Christians: What particular rules have you in order to grow in grace? What arts of holy living?

2. As Methodists: Do you never miss your class?

3. As Preachers: Have you thoroughly considered your duty? And do you make a conscience of executing every part of it? Do you meet every society and their leaders?

These means may be used without fruit. But there are some means which cannot: namely, watching, denying ourselves, taking up our cross, exercise of the presence of God.

1. Do you steadily watch against the world? Yourself? Your besetting sin?

2. Do you deny yourself every useless pleasure of sense? Imagination? Honor? Are you temperate in all things? Instance in food: (1) Do you use only that kind and that degree which is best both for body and soul? Do you see the necessity of this? (2) Do you eat no more at each meal than is necessary? Are you not heavy or drowsy after dinner? (3) Do you use only that kind, and that degree of drink, which is best both for your body and soul? (4) Do you choose and use water for your common drink? And only take wine medicinally or sacramentally?

3. Wherein do you take up your cross daily? Do you cheerfully bear your cross,

however grievous to nature, as a gift of God, and labor to profit thereby?

4. Do you endeavor to set God always before you? To see his eye continually fixed upon you?

Never can you use these means but a blessing will ensue. And the more you use them, the more you will grow in grace.

SECTION IV.

The Necessity of Union among ourselves.

Let us be deeply sensible (from what we have known) of the evil of a division in principle, spirit, or practice, and the dreadful consequences to ourselves and others. If we are united, what can stand before us? If we divide, we shall destroy ourselves, the work of God, and the souls of our people.

Quest. What can be done in order to a closer union with each other?

Answ. 1. Let us be deeply convinced of the absolute necessity of it.

2. Pray earnestly for, and speak freely to each other.

3. When we meet, let us never part without prayer.

4. Take great care not to despise each other's gifts.

5. Never speak lightly of each other.

6. Let us defend each other's character in everything so far as is consistent with truth.

7. Labor in honor each to prefer the other before himself.

8. We recommend a serious perusal of *The Causes, Evils, and Cures of Heart and Church Divisions.*

SECTION V.

How we can Employ our Time profitably, when not Traveling, or engaged in Public Exercises.

Quest. 1. What general method of employing our time shall we advise?

Answ. We advise you, 1. As often as possible to rise at four. 2. From four to five in the morning, and from five to six in the evening, to meditate, pray, and read the Scriptures with notes, and the closely practical parts of what Mr. Wesley has published. 3. From six in the morning till twelve, wherever it is practicable, let the time be spent in appropriate reading, study, and private devotion.

Quest. 2. Why is it that the people under our care are not better?

Answ. Other reasons may concur, but the chief is, because we are not more knowing and more holy.

Quest. 3. But why are we not more knowing?

Answ. Because we are idle. We forget our first rule: "Be diligent. Never be unemployed. Never be triflingly employed. Neither spend any more time at any place than is strictly necessary." We fear there is altogether a fault in this matter, and that few of us are clear. Which of us spend as many hours a day in God's work as we did formerly in man's work? We talk—talk or read what comes next to hand. We must, absolutely must, cure this evil, or betray the cause of God. But how? 1. Read the most useful books, and that regularly and constantly. 2. Steadily spend all the morning in this employment, or at least five hours in the four and twenty. "But I have no taste for reading." Contract a taste for it by use, or return to your former employment. "But I have no books." Be diligent to spread the books, and you will have the use of them.

SECTION VI.

The Matter and Manner of Preaching.

Quest. 1. What is the best general method of preaching?

Answ. 1. To convince: 2. To offer Christ: 3. To invite: [illegible] To build up: And to do this in some measure in every sermon.

Quest. 2. What is the most effectual way of preaching Christ?

Answ. The most effectual way of preaching Christ is, to preach him in all his offices; and to declare his law, as well as his Gospel, both to believers and unbelievers. Let us strongly and closely insist upon inward and outward holiness in all its branches.

SECTION VII.

Rules by which we should continue, or desist from Preaching at any Place.

Quest. 1. Is it advisable for us to preach in as many places as we can without forming any societies?

Answ. By no means. We have made the trial in various places, and that for a considerable time. But all the seed has fallen by the way-side. There is scarce any fruit remaining.

Quest. 2. Where should we endeavor to preach most?

Answ. 1. Where there is the greatest number of quiet and willing hearers.

2. Where there is most fruit.

Quest. 3. Ought we not diligently to observe in what places God is pleased at any time to pour out his Spirit more abundantly?

Answ. We ought: and at that time to send more laborers than usual into that part of the harvest.

SECTION VIII.

Visiting from House to House, guarding against those Things that are so common to Professors, and enforcing Practical Religion.

Quest. 1. How can we further assist those under our care?

Answ. By instructing them at their own houses. What unspeakable need is there of this! The world says, "*The Methodists are no better than other people.*" This is not true in the general: but, 1. Personal religion, either toward God or man, is too superficial among us. We can but just touch on a few particulars. How little faith is there among us! How little communion with God! How little living in heaven, walking in eternity, deadness to every creature! How much love of the world! Desire of pleasure, of ease, of getting money! How little brotherly love! What continual judging one another! What gossiping, evil-speaking, tale-bearing! What want of moral honesty! To instance only one particular: Who does as he would be done by in buying and selling?

2. Family religion is wanting in many branches. And what avails public preaching alone, though we could preach like angels? We must, yea, every traveling preacher must instruct the people from house to house. Till this be done, and that in good earnest, Methodists will be no better.

Our religion is not sufficiently deep, universal, uniform; but superficial, partial, uneven. It will be so till we spend half as much time in this visiting as we now do in talking uselessly. Can we find a better method of doing this than Mr. Baxter's? If not, let us adopt it without delay. His whole tract, entitled, *Gildas Silvianus; or, The Reformed Pastor*, is well worth a careful perusal. Speaking of this visiting from house to house, he says, (p. 351,) "We shall find many hinderances, both in ourselves and the people."

1. In ourselves there is much dullness and laziness, so that there will be much ado to get us to be faithful in the work.

2. We have a base, man-pleasing temper, so that we let them perish rather than lose their love; we let them go quietly to hell lest we should offend them.

3. Some of us have a foolish bashfulness. We know not how to begin, and blush to contradict the devil.

4. But the greater hinderance is weakness of faith. Our whole motion is weak, because the spring of it is weak.

5. Lastly, we are unskillful in the work. How few know how to deal with men, so as to get within them, and suit all our discourse to their several conditions and tempers: to choose the fittest subjects, and follow them with a holy mixture of seriousness, terror, love, and meekness!

But undoubtedly this private application is implied in those solemn words of the apostle: "I charge thee before God and the Lord Jesus Christ, who shall judge the quick and the dead at his appearing, preach the word: be instant in season, out of season: reprove, rebuke, exhort, with all long-suffering."

O brethren, if we could but set this work on foot in all our societies, and prosecute it zealously, what glory would redound to God! If the common lukewarmness were banished, and every shop, and every house, busied in speaking of the word and works of God, surely God would dwell in our habitations, and make us his delight.

And this is absolutely necessary to the welfare of our people, some of whom neither repent nor believe to this day. Look round, and see how many of them are still in apparent danger of damnation. And how can you walk and talk, and be merry with such people, when you know their case? When you look them in the face, you should break forth into tears, as the prophet did when he looked upon Hazael, and then set on them with the most vehement exhortations. O, for God's sake, and the sake of poor souls, bestir yourselves, and spare no pains that may conduce to their salvation!

What cause have we to bleed before the Lord that we have so long neglected this good work! If we had but engaged in it sooner, how many more might have been brought to Christ! And how much holier and happier might our societies have been before now! And why might we not have done it sooner? There were many hinderances; and so there always will be. But the greatest hinderance is in ourselves, in our littleness of faith and love.

But it is objected, I. "This will take up so much time, we shall not have leisure to follow our studies." We answer, 1. Gaining knowledge is a good thing, but saving souls is a better. 2. By this very thing you will gain the most excellent knowledge, that of God and eternity. 3. You will have time for gaining other knowledge too. Only sleep no more than you need; "and never be idle, or triflingly employed." But, 4. If you can do but one, let your studies alone. We ought to throw by all the libraries in the world, rather than be guilty of the loss of one soul.

It is objected, II. "The people will not submit to it." If some will not, others will. And the success with them will repay all your labor. O let us herein follow the example of St. Paul! 1. For our general business, *Serving the Lord with all hu-*

mility of mind: 2. Our special work, *Take heed to yourselves, and to all the flock:* 3. Our doctrine, *Repentance toward God, and faith toward our Lord Jesus Christ:* 4. The place, *I have taught you publicly, and from house to house:* 5. The object and manner of teaching, *I ceased not to warn every one, night and day, with tears:* 6. His innocence and self-denial herein, *I have coveted no man's silver or gold:* 7. His patience, *Neither count I my life dear unto myself.* And among all other motives let these be ever before our eyes: 1. *The Church of God, which he hath purchased with his own blood:* 2. *Grievous wolves shall enter in; yea, of yourselves shall men arise, speaking perverse things.*

Write this upon your hearts, and it will do you more good than twenty years' study. Then you will have no time to spare: you will have work enough. Then likewise no preacher will stay with us who is as salt that has lost its savor. For to such this employment would be mere drudgery. And in order to it, you will have need of all the knowledge you can procure, and grace you can attain.

The sum is, Go into every house in course, and teach every one therein, young and old, to be Christians inwardly and outwardly; make every particular plain to their understandings; fix it in their minds; write it on their hearts. In order to this, there must be line upon line, precept upon precept. What patience, what love, what knowledge, is requisite for this! We must needs do this, were it only to avoid idleness. Do we not loiter away many hours in every week? Each try himself: no idleness is consistent with a growth in grace. Nay, without exactness in redeeming time, you cannot retain the grace you receive in justification.

Quest. 2. Why are we not more holy? Why do we not live in eternity? Walk with God all the day long? Why are we not all devoted to God? Breathing the whole spirit of missionaries?

Ans. Chiefly because we are enthusiasts; looking for the end without using the means. To touch only upon two or three instances: Who of us rises at four, or even at five, when we do not preach? Do we know the obligation and benefit of fasting or abstinence? How often do we practice it? The neglect of this alone is sufficient to account for our feebleness and faintness of spirit. We are continually grieving the

Holy Spirit of God by the habitual neglect of a plain duty. Let us amend from this hour.

Quest. 3. How shall we guard against Sabbath-breaking, evil-speaking, unprofitable conversation, lightness, expensiveness or gayety of apparel, and contracting debts without due care to discharge them?

Ans. 1. Let us preach expressly on each of these heads. 2. Read in every society the sermon on evil-speaking. 3. Let the leaders closely examine and exhort every person to put away the accursed thing. 4. Let the preachers warn every society that none who is guilty herein can remain with us. 5. Extirpate buying or selling goods which have not paid the duty laid upon them by government, out of our Church. Let none remain with us who will not totally abstain from this evil in every kind and degree. Extirpate bribery, receiving anything, directly or indirectly, for voting at any election. Show no respect to persons herein, but expel all that touch the accursed thing. And strongly advise our people to discountenance all treats given by candidates before or at elections, and not to be partakers, in any respect, of such iniquitous practices.

SECTION IX.

The Method of Receiving Traveling Preachers on Trial.

Quest. How is a Preacher to be received on trial?

Ans. 1. By the Annual Conference.

2. In the interval of the Conference, by a Bishop, or the Presiding Elder of the district, until the sitting of the Conference.

But no one shall be received unless he first procure a recommendation from the Quarterly Conference of his circuit or station. We may then, if he give us satisfaction, receive him on trial. But before any such candidate is received on trial, or into full connection, or ordained Deacon or Elder, he shall give satisfactory evidence respecting his knowledge of those particular subjects which have been recommended to his consideration.

When a Preacher's name is not printed in the Minutes, he must receive a written license from a Bishop or Presiding Elder.

Observe! taking on trial is entirely different from admitting a Preacher into full connection. One on trial may be either admitted or rejected, without doing him any wrong: otherwise it would be no trial at all.

At each Annual Conference, those who are received on trial, or are admitted into full connection, shall be asked whether they are willing to devote themselves to the missionary work; and a list of the names of all those who are willing to do so shall be taken and reported to the Corresponding Secretary of the Missionary Society; and all such shall be considered as ready and willing to be employed as missionaries whenever called for by either of the Bishops.

SECTION X.

The Manner of Receiving Traveling Preachers into Full Connection.

Quest. What method do we use in receiving a Preacher at the Conference into full connection?

Answ. After solemn fasting and prayer, every person proposed shall then be asked, before the Conference, the following questions, (with any others which may be thought necessary,) namely: Have you faith in Christ? Are you going on to perfection? Do you expect to be made perfect in love in this life? Are you groaning after it? Are you resolved to devote your self wholly to God and his work? Do you know the rules of society? Do you keep them? Do you constantly attend the sacrament? Have you read the form of Discipline? Are you willing to conform to it? Have you considered the rules of a Preacher, (see § 2, p. 60,) especially the first, tenth, and twelfth? Will you keep them for conscience' sake? Are you determined to employ all your time in the work of God? Will you endeavor not to speak too long or too loud? Will you diligently instruct the children in every place? Will you visit from house to house? Will you recommend fasting, or abstinence, both by precept and example? Are you in debt?

Then if he give us satisfaction, after he has been employed two successive years in the regular itinerant work on circuits, in stations, or in our institutions of learning, which is to commence from his being received on trial at the Annual Conference, and being approved by the Annual Conference, and examined by the President of the Conference, he may be received into full connection.

N. B. A Missionary employed on a Foreign Mission may be admitted into full connection, if recommended by the Superintendent of the Mission where he labors, without being present at the Annual Conference for examination.

SECTION XI.

The Reception of Preachers from the Wesleyan Connection, and from other Denominations.

Quest. 1. In what manner shall we receive those ministers who may come to us from the Wesleyan connection in Europe or Canada?

Answ. If they come to us properly accredited from either the British, Irish, or Canada Conference, they may be received according to such credentials, provided they give satisfaction to an Annual Conference of their willingness to conform to our Church government and usages.

Quest. 2. How shall we receive those ministers who may offer to unite with us from other Christian Churches?

Answ. Those ministers of other evangelical Churches, who may desire to unite with our Church, whether as local or itinerant, may be received according to our usages, on condition of their taking upon them our ordination vows, without the reimposition of hands, giving satisfaction to an Annual Conference of their being in orders, and of their agreement with us in doctrine, discipline, government, and usages; *provided* the Conference is also satisfied with their gifts, grace, and usefulness. Whenever any such minister is received, he shall be furnished with a certificate, signed by one of our Bishops, in the following words, namely:

This is to certify, that has been admitted into Conference as a Traveling Preacher, [or has been admitted as a Local Preacher on circuit,] he having been ordained to the office of Deacon, [or an Elder, as the case may be,] according to the usages of the Church, of which he has been a member and minister; and he is hereby authorized to exercise the functions pertaining to his office in the Methodist Episcopal Church, so long as his life and conversation are such as become the Gospel of Christ.

Given under my hand and seal, at this day of , in the year of our Lord

Quest. 3. How shall we receive Preachers of other denominations who are not in orders?

Answ. They may be received as licentiates, provided they give satisfaction to a Quarterly or an Annual Conference that they are suitable persons to exercise the office, and of their agreement with the doctrines, discipline, government, and usages of our Church.

SECTION XII.

The Duties of those who have the Charge of Circuits or Stations.

Quest. 1. What are the duties of the Elder, Deacon, or Preacher who has the special charge of a circuit?

Answ. 1. To see that the other Preachers in his circuit behave well, and want nothing.

2. To renew the tickets for the admission of members into love-feast quarterly.

3. To meet the Stewards and Leaders as often as possible. To hear reports from leaders of any that are sick, of any that walk disorderly and will not be reproved, or of any that willfully neglect the means of grace.

The Leaders' Meeting may recommend proper persons for admission into full connection; to recommend proper persons for license to exhort, or for license to preach; also to hear reports from the Stewards.

4. To appoint all the Leaders, to change them when he sees it necessary, and to examine each of them, with all possible exactness, at least once a quarter, concerning his method of meeting a class.

5. To receive, try, and expel members, according to the form of Discipline.

6. To hold watch-nights and love-feasts.

7. To hold quarterly meetings in the absence of the Presiding Elder.

8. To take care that every society be duly supplied with books.

9. To take an exact account of all the matters specified in part ii, chap. i, § 3, and report them to the Annual Conference, that their number may be printed in the Minutes.

10. To give an account of his circuit every quarter to his Presiding Elder.

11. To report at each quarterly meeting the names of those who have been received into the Church or excluded therefrom during the quarter; also the names of those who have been received or dismissed by certificate, and of those who have died or have withdrawn from our Church.

12. To examine the accounts of all the Stewards.

13. To appoint a person to receive the quarterly collection in the *classes.*

14. To see that *public* collections be made quarterly, if need be.

15. To encourage the support of missions* and Sunday-schools, and the publication and distribution of Bibles, tracts,† and Sunday-school books, by forming societies and making collections for these objects in such way and manner as the Annual Conference to which he belongs shall from time to time direct.

16. To publicly catechise the children in the Sunday-school and at special meetings appointed for that purpose. It shall also be the duty of each Preacher, in his report to each Quarterly Conference, to state to what extent he has publicly or privately catechised the children of his charge.

17. To form Bible classes for the larger children, youth, and adults; to attend to all the duties prescribed for the training of children in part i, chap. i, § 3 and part iv, § 1.

18. If the Annual Conference to which he belongs should not give any directions on the subject, to take up a collection in the course of the year, or raise a subscrip-

* See part iv, § 2. † See part iv, §§ 1 and 5.

tion, as he may judge expedient, the proceeds of which shall be at his disposal in the purchase and distribution of tracts.

19. To lay before the Quarterly Conference, at each quarterly meeting, as far as practicable, to be entered on its journal, a written statement of the number and state of the Sunday-schools in the circuit or station, and to report the same to his Annual Conference according to the form published by the Sunday-School Union of the Methodist Episcopal Church, together with the amount raised for the support of missions, and for the publication of Bibles and tracts.

20. To take an annual collection in each of his appointments in behalf of the Sunday-School Union.

21. To raise a yearly subscription in those circuits that can bear it, for building churches and paying the debts of those which have been already erected.

22. To choose a committee of lay members to make a just application of the money where it is most wanted.

Quest. 2. What other directions shall we give him?

Answ. Several.

1. To take a regular catalogue of the

societies in towns and cities, as they live in the streets.

2. To leave his successor a particular account of the circuit, including an account of the subscribers for our periodicals.

3. To enforce vigorously, but calmly, all the rules of the society.

4. To suffer no love-feast to last above an hour and a half.

5. To warn all from time to time that none are to remove from one circuit to another without a note of recommendation from the preacher of the circuit in these words: "*A. B., the bearer, has been an acceptable member of the Methodist Episcopal Church.*" And to inform them that, without such a certificate, they will not be received into the Church in other places.

6. To recommend everywhere decency and cleanliness.

7. To read the rules of the society, with the aid of the other preachers, once a year in every congregation, and once a quarter in every society.

8. The Preacher who has the charge of a circuit shall appoint prayer-meetings wherever he can in his circuit.

9. Wherever it is practicable he shall so arrange the appointments as to give the

Local Preachers regular and systematic employment on the Sabbath.

10. He shall take care that a fast be held in every society in his circuit on the Friday preceding every quarterly meeting, and that a memorandum of it be written on all the class papers.

11. To license such persons as he may judge proper to officiate as exhorters in the Church, provided no person shall be so licensed without the consent of the Leaders' Meeting, or of the class of which he is a member, where no Leaders' Meeting is held; and the exhorters so authorized shall be subject to the annual examination of character in the Quarterly Conference, and have their license annually renewed by the Presiding Elder, or the Preacher having the charge, if approved by the Quarterly Conference.

Quest. 3. What can be done to supply the circuits during the sittings of the Conferences?

Answ. 1. Let all the appointments stand according to the plan of the circuit.

2. Engage as many Local Preachers and exhorters as will supply them, and let them be paid for their time in proportion to the allowance of the Traveling Preachers.

3. If Preachers and exhorters cannot attend let some person of ability be appointed in every society to sing, pray, and read one of Mr. Wesley's sermons.

4. But if that cannot be done let there be prayer-meetings.

N. B. The Preachers who have the oversight of circuits are required to execute all our rules fully and strenuously against all frauds, and particularly against dishonest insolvencies, suffering none to remain in our Church on any account who are found guilty of any fraud.

☞ For the mode of procedure in case of insolvency of members, and in settling disputes, etc., as to the payment of debts or otherwise, see part ii, chap. x, § 2, item 6.

CHAPTER III.

OF BISHOPS.

SECTION I.

The Election of Bishops, and their Duty.

Quest. 1. How is a Bishop to be constituted?

Answ. By the election of the General Conference, and the laying on of the hands of three Bishops, or at least of one Bishop and two Elders. But the General Conference may authorize the election of a Missionary Bishop in the interim of the General Conference.

Quest. 2. If by death, expulsion, or otherwise, there be no Bishop remaining in our Church, what shall we do?

Answ. The General Conference shall elect a Bishop, and the elders, or any three of them, who shall be appointed by the General Conference for that purpose, shall ordain him according to our form of ordination.

Quest. 3. What are the duties of a Bishop?

Answ. 1. To preside in our Conferences.

2. To form the districts according to his judgment.

3. To fix the appointments of the Preachers, provided he shall not allow any Preacher to remain in the same station more than two years successively; except the Presiding Elders, the Corresponding Secretary and Assistant Corresponding Secretary of the Missionary Society, the Editors and Agents at New York and Cincinnati; the Editors at Auburn, Pittsburgh, Chicago, St. Louis, Portland, and San Francisco; the Superannuated, and Worn-out Preachers; missionaries among the Indians, Welsh, Swedes, Norwegians, and other missionaries among foreigners, (not including the Germans,) where supplies are difficult to be obtained; missionaries to our people of color and on foreign stations; chaplains to state prisons and in the army or navy; those Preachers who may be appointed to labor for the special benefit of seamen, and for the American Bible Society, or for any State Bible Society auxiliary thereto; the presidents, principals, or teachers of seminaries of learning, which are, or may be under our superintendence; or the Preacher stationed at Five Points Mission

in New York, or at the American Chapel in Paris; and also, when requested by an Annual Conference, to appoint a Preacher for a longer time than two years to any seminary of learning not under our care: *provided*, also, that, with the exceptions above named, he shall not continue a preacher in the same appointment more than two years in six. He shall have authority, when requested by an Annual Conference, to appoint an agent, whose duty it shall be to travel throughout the bounds of such Conference, for the purpose of establishing and aiding Sabbath-schools, and distributing Tracts, and also to appoint an agent or agents for the benefit of our literary institutions, and an agent for the German publishing fund.

4. In the intervals of the Conferences, to change, receive, and suspend Preachers, as necessity may require, and as the Discipline directs.

5. To travel through the connection at large.

6. To oversee the spiritual and temporal business of our Church.

7. To ordain Bishops, Elders, and Deacons.

8. To decide all questions of law in an

Annual Conference, subject to an appeal to the General Conference; but in all cases the application of law shall be with the Conference.

9. To prescribe a Course of Study in English literature and in science, upon which those applying for admission upon trial in the Annual Conferences shall be examined and approved before such admission; and also to prescribe a course of reading and study proper to be pursued by candidates for the ministry for the term of four years.

10. A Bishop may, when he judges it necessary, unite two or more circuits or stations for Quarterly Conference purposes, without affecting their separate financial interests or pastoral duties.

Quest. 4. If a Bishop cease from traveling at large among the people, shall he still exercise his episcopal office among us in any degree?

Answ. If he cease from traveling without the consent of the General Conference, he shall not thereafter exercise the episcopal office in our Church.

Quest. 5. What shall be done when there is no Bishop to travel at large?

Answ. In case there be no Bishop to travel through the districts and exercise the episcopal office, on account of death, or otherwise, the districts shall be regulated in every respect by the Annual Conferences and the Presiding Elders in the interval of General Conference, ordination excepted.

SECTION II.

The Trial of a Bishop.

Quest. 1. To whom is a Bishop amenable for his conduct?

Answ. To the General Conference, who have power to expel him for improper conduct, if they see it necessary.

Quest. 2. What provision shall be made for the trial of a Bishop, if he should be accused of immorality in the interval of the General Conference?

Answ. If a Bishop be accused of immorality, three Traveling Elders shall call upon him, and examine him on the subject; and if the three Elders verily believe that the Bishop is guilty of the crime, they shall call to their aid two Presiding Elders from two districts in the neighborhood of that where the crime was committed, each of which Presiding Elders shall bring with him two Elders, or an Elder and a Deacon.

The above-mentioned nine persons shall form a Conference, to examine into the charge brought against the Bishop; and if two thirds of them verily believe him to be guilty of the crime laid to his charge, they shall have authority to suspend the Bishop till the ensuing General Conference, and the districts shall be regulated in the mean time as is provided in part ii, ch. i, § 3, and part ii, ch. iv, § 1; but no accusation shall be received against a Bishop except it be delivered in writing, signed by those who are to prove the crime; and a copy of the accusation shall be given to the accused Bishop.

SECTION III.

The support of Bishops, and the Families of Deceased Bishops.

Quest. What provision shall be made for the support of our Bishops, and the widows and children of deceased Bishops?

Answ. It shall be the duty of each Annual Conference within whose bounds a Bishop, or the widow or child of a deceased Bishop may reside, to appoint a committee, whose duty it shall be to make an estimate of the amount necessary to furnish a comfortable support to such Bishop, considering the number and condition of his family, and the amount necessary to assist such widow or child in obtaining a comfortable support, which estimates shall be subject to the action of the Conference, and the bishops are authorized to draw on the funds of the Book Concern for said amount allowed them, and also for the amount of their traveling expenses.

The Bishop presiding at an Annual Conference where an estimate is made for the widow or orphan of a deceased Bishop, shall be authorized to draw on the Book Concern for such amount.

CHAPTER IV.

PRESIDING ELDERS.

SECTION I.

Presiding Elders and their Duty.

Quest. 1. By whom are the Presiding Elders to be chosen?

Answ. By the Bishops.

Quest. 2. By whom are the Presiding Elders to be stationed and changed?

Answ. By the Bishops.

Quest. 3. How long may a Bishop allow an Elder to preside in the same district?

Answ. For any term not exceeding four years; after which he shall not be appointed to the same district for six years.

Quest. 4. What are the duties of a Presiding Elder?

Answ. 1. To travel through his appointed district.

2. In the absence of the Bishop, to take charge of all the Elders and Deacons, Traveling and Local Preachers, and exhorters in his district.

3. To change, receive, and suspend Preachers in his district during the intervals of the Conferences, and in the absence of the Bishop, as the Discipline directs.

4. In the absence of a Bishop, to preside in the Conference.*

5. To be present at, as far as practicable, and to hold all the quarterly meetings; and to call together at each quarterly meeting a Quarterly Conference, consisting of all the Traveling and Local Preachers, exhorters, stewards, and leaders of the circuit or station, and the first male superintendents of our Sunday-schools, being members of our Church, and approved by the Quarterly Conference, and none else, to hear complaints, and to receive and try appeals, and to transact such other business as is provided for in part ii, ch. i, § 4.

6. To oversee the spiritual and temporal business of the Church in his district, and to promote, by all proper means, the cause of Missions† and Sunday-schools, and the publication, at our own press, of Bibles, Tracts, and Sunday-school Books; and carefully to inquire, at each Quarterly Conference, whether the rules respecting the instruction of children have been faithfully

* See pt. ii, ch. i, § 3. † See pt. iv, § 2, it. 13.

observed; and to report to the Annual Conference the names of all Traveling Preachers within his district who shall neglect to observe these rules.

7. To take care that every part of our Discipline be enforced in his district; and to decide all questions of law in a Quarterly Conference, subject to an appeal to the President of the next Annual Conference; but in all cases the application of law shall be with the Conference.

8. To attend the Bishops when present in his district; and to give them, when absent, all necessary information, by letter, of the state of his district.

9. To direct the candidates who are admitted on trial to those studies which have been recommended by the Bishops.

10. To explain to those Preachers who are on trial, as well as to those who are in future to be proposed for trial, that they may be either admitted or rejected without doing them any wrong.

11. If any Preacher absent himself from his circuit, the Presiding Elder shall, as far as possible, fill his place with another Preacher, who shall be paid for his labors out of the allowance of the absent Preacher, in proportion to his usual allowance.

Quest. 5. Shall the Presiding Elder have power to employ a Preacher who has been rejected at the previous Annual Conference?

Answ. He shall not, unless the Conference should give him liberty, under certain conditions.

SECTION II.

The Presiding Elder's Support.

Quest. How shall the Presiding Elders be supported?

Answ. There shall be annually, in every district, a meeting composed of one steward from each circuit and station, to be selected by the Quarterly Conference, whose duty it shall be, with the advice of the Presiding Elder, (who shall preside in such meeting,) to make an estimate of the amount necessary to furnish a comfortable support to the Presiding Elder, and to apportion the same, including house rent and traveling expenses, among the different circuits and stations in the district, according to their several ability; and in all cases the Presiding Elder shall share with the preachers in his district in proportion with what they have respectively received; but if there be a surplus of money raised for the support of the preachers in one or more of the circuits or stations in his district, he shall receive such surplus, provided he do not receive more than his allowance.

[N. B.—For the method of proceeding against an accused Presiding Elder, see part ii, chap. v, sec. 2, p. 105.—ED.]

CHAPTER V.

TRAVELING ELDERS.

SECTION I.

The Election of Traveling Elders, and their Duty.

Quest. 1. How is an Elder constituted?

Answ. By the election of a majority of the Annual Conference, and by the laying on of the hands of a Bishop and some of the Elders that are present.

Quest. 2. What is the duty of a Traveling Elder?

Answ. 1. To administer Baptism and the Lord's Supper, to solemnize matrimony, and to conduct Divine worship.

2. To do all the duties of a traveling preacher.

No Elder that ceases to travel, without the consent of the Annual Conference, certified under the hand of the President of the Conference, except in case of sickness, debility, or other unavoidable circumstances, shall on any account exercise the peculiar functions of his office, or even be allowed to preach among us: *nevertheless,* the final determination in all such cases is with the Annual Conference.

Quest. 3. What shall be the time of probation of a Traveling Deacon for the office of an Elder?

Answ. Every Traveling Deacon shall exercise that office for two years, before he be eligible to the office of Elder; except in the case of missions, when the Annual Conferences shall have authority to elect for the Elder's office sooner, if they judge it expedient.

When a preacher shall have passed his examination, and been admitted into full connection, and elected to Deacon's office, but fails of his ordination through the absence of the Bishop, his eligibility to the office of Elder shall run from the time of his election to the office of a Deacon.

SECTION II.

The Method of Proceeding against accused Traveling Ministers or Preachers.

Quest. 1. What shall be done when an Elder, Deacon, or Preacher is under report of being guilty of *some crime* expressly forbidden in the word of God, as an unchristian practice, sufficient to exclude a person from the kingdom of grace and glory?

Answ. 1. In the interval of the Annual Conference, let the Presiding Elder, in the absence of a Bishop, call as many traveling ministers as he shall think fit, at least three; and, if possible, bring the accused and the accuser face to face; and cause a correct record of the investigation to be kept and transmitted to the Annual Conference. If the person be clearly convicted, he shall be suspended from all ministerial services and Church privileges until the ensuing Annual Conference, at which his case shall be fully considered and determined. But if the accused be a Presiding Elder, three of the senior preachers of his district shall inquire into the character of the report, and if they judge it necessary, call in the Presiding Elder of any adjoining district, who shall appoint a Committee of five Elders from within the bounds of the Annual Conference of which the accused is a member, and also preside at the examination.

If the accused and accuser cannot be brought face to face, but the supposed delinquent flees from trial, it shall be received as a presumptive proof of guilt; and out of the mouth of two or three witnesses he shall be condemned. Nevertheless, even in that case, the Annual Conference shall reconsider and determine the whole matter.

And if the accused be a superannuated preacher, living out of the bounds of the Conference of which he is a member, he shall be held responsible to the Annual Conference within whose bounds he may reside, who shall have power to try, acquit, suspend, locate, or expel him, in the same manner as if he were a member of said Conference.

When a member of an Annual Conference is accused of crime in the interval of his Conference sessions, and is suspended by a committee, and subsequently convicted by his Conference, and expelled, his claim upon the funds of the Conference shall cease from the time of his suspension.

2. If the charge be preferred at the Conference, the case may be referred to a committee, in the presence of a Presiding Elder, or a member appointed by the Bishop in his stead, who shall cause a faithful record of the proceedings and testimony to be laid before the Conference; on which, with such other evidence as may be admitted, the case shall be decided.

Quest. 2. What shall be done in cases of improper tempers, words, or actions?

Answ. The person so offending shall be reprehended by his senior in office. Should a second transgression take place, one, two, or three ministers or preachers are to be taken as witnesses. If he be not then cured, he shall be tried at the next Annual Conference, and, if found guilty and impenitent, shall be expelled from the connection, and his name so returned in the Minutes of the Conference.

Quest. 3. What shall be done when a member of an Annual Conference fails in business, or contracts debts which he is not able to pay?

Answ. Let the Presiding Elder appoint three judicious members of the Church to inspect the accounts, contracts, and circumstances of the supposed delinquent, and if, in their opinion, he has behaved dishonestly, or contracted debts without the probability of paying, let the case be disposed of according to the answer of question one of this section.

Quest. 4. What shall be done with those ministers or preachers who hold and disseminate, publicly or privately, doctrines which are contrary to our Articles of Religion?

Answ. Let the same process be observed as in case of gross immorality: but if the minister or preacher so offending do solemnly engage not to disseminate such erroneous doctrines in public or in private, he shall be borne with, till his case be laid before the next Annual Conference, which shall determine the matter.

Quest. 5. What shall be done when a traveling minister is accused of being so unacceptable, inefficient, or secular, as to be no longer useful in his work?

Answ. The Conference shall investigate the case, and if it appear that the complaint is well founded, and the accused will not voluntarily retire, the Conference may locate him without his consent.

But should the Conference, having jurisdiction in any of the foregoing cases, judge it expedient to try the accused by a select number, it may appoint not less than nine, nor more than fifteen, of its members for that purpose, who, in the presence of a Bishop or a chairman, which the President of the Conference shall appoint, and one or more of the Secretaries of the Conference, shall have full power to consider and determine the case according to the rules which govern Annual Conferences in such proceedings, and they shall make a faithful report of all their doings to the Secretary of the Conference in writing, and deliver up to him the bill of charges, the evidence taken, and the decision rendered, with all other documents brought into the trial.

Provided, nevertheless, that in all the above-mentioned cases of trial, and conviction, an appeal to the ensuing General Conference shall be allowed, if the condemned person signify his intention to appeal, at the time of his condemnation, or at any time thereafter when he is informed thereof.

In all the above-mentioned cases it shall be the duty of the Secretary of the Annual Conference carefully to preserve the Minutes of the trial, whether taken before a committee or before the Conference, and all the documents relating to the case, together with the charge or charges, and the specification or specifications; which Minutes and documents only, in case of an appeal from the decision of an Annual Conference, shall be presented to the General Conference in evidence on the case. And in all cases, when an appeal is made, and admitted by the General Conference, the appellant shall either state personally, or by his representative, (who shall be a member of the Conference,) the grounds of his appeal, showing cause why he appeals, and he shall be allowed to make his defense without interruption. After which, the representatives of the Annual Conference from whose decision the appeal is made, shall be permitted to respond in presence of the appellant, who shall have the privilege of replying to such representatives, which shall close the pleadings on both sides. This done, the appellant shall withdraw, and the Conference or Committee on the case shall decide. And after such form of trial and expulsion, the person so expelled shall have no privileges of society or sacraments in our Church, without confession, contrition, and satisfactory reformation.

A Preacher on trial who may be accused of crime shall be accountable to the Quarterly Conference of the circuit on which he travels. The Presiding Elder shall call a committee of three Local Preachers, who may suspend him; and the Quarterly Conference may expel him: *nevertheless*, he shall have a right to an appeal to the next Annual Conference.

When any Traveling Elder or Deacon is deprived of his credentials, by expulsion or otherwise, they shall be filed with the papers of the Annual Conference of which he was a member; and should he at any future time give satisfactory evidence to said Conference of his amendment, and procure a certificate of the Quarterly Conference of the circuit or station where he resides, or of an Annual Conference who may have admitted him on trial, recommending to the Annual Conference of which he *was* a member formerly, the restoration of his credentials, the said Conference may restore them.

CHAPTER VI.

TRAVELING DEACONS.

The Election of Traveling Deacons, and their Duty.

Quest. 1. How is a Traveling Deacon constituted?

Answ. By the election of a majority of the Annual Conference, and the laying on of the hands of a Bishop.

Quest. 2. What is the duty of a Traveling Deacon?

Answ. 1. To administer Baptism, and to solemnize Matrimony.

2. To assist the Elder in administering the Lord's Supper.

3. To do all the duties of a Traveling Preacher.

N. B. Whenever a Preacher on trial is selected by the Bishop for a mission, he may, if elected by an Annual Conference, ordain him a Deacon before his probation ends.

No Deacon who ceases to travel without the consent of the Annual Conference, certified under the hand of the President of the Conference, except in case of sickness, debility, or other unavoidable circumstances, shall on any account exercise the peculiar functions of his office, or even be allowed to preach among us: *nevertheless*, the final determination in all such cases is with the Annual Conference.

[N. B.—For trial of Deacons, see part ii, chap. v, sec. 2.

For the support of Deacons, see part ii, chap. i, sec. 4.—ED.]

CHAPTER VII.

SUPERANNUATED OR WORN-OUT PREACHERS.

SECTION I.

The Rights and Privileges of Superannuated Preachers who may live without the Bounds of their own Conference.

EVERY Superannuated Preacher, who may reside without the bounds of the Conference of which he is a member, shall have a seat in the Quarterly Conference, and all the privileges of membership in the Church where he may reside; and he shall annually forward to his Conference a certificate of his Christian and ministerial conduct, together with an account of the number and circumstances of his family, signed by the Presiding Elder of the district, or the Preacher in charge of the circuit or station within whose bounds he may reside; without which the Conference shall not be required to allow his claim.

[N. B.—For support of Superannuated Preachers, see duties of Quarterly Conference, quest. 4, answ. 10.

For the trial of a Superannuated Preacher, see part ii, chap. v, sec. 2.—ED.]

CHAPTER VIII.

LOCAL PREACHERS.

SECTION I.

General Directions concerning Local Preachers.

Quest. What directions shall be given concerning Local Preachers?

Answ. The Quarterly Conference shall have authority to license proper persons to preach, and renew their license annually, when, in the judgment of said Conference, their gifts, grace, and usefulness will warrant such renewal; to recommend suitable candidates to the Annual Conference for Deacons' or Elders' orders in the local connection, for admission on trial in the traveling connection; and to try, suspend, expel, or acquit any Local Preacher in the circuit or station, against whom charges may be brought. *Provided*, that no person shall be licensed to preach without the recommendation of the society of which he is a member, or of a Leaders' Meeting. Nor shall any one be licensed to preach, or recommended to the Annual Conference to travel, or for ordination, without first being examined in the Quarterly Conference on the subject of doctrines and discipline.

SECTION II.

Local Preachers and their Ordination.

1. A licensed Local Preacher shall be eligible to the office of a Deacon, after he has preached four years from the time he received a regular license, and has obtained a testimonial from the Quarterly Conference, after proper examination, signed by the President, and countersigned by the Secretary; and after his character has passed in examination before, and he has obtained the approbation of, the Annual Conference.

2. A Local Deacon shall be eligible to the office of an Elder, after he has preached four years from the time he was ordained a Deacon, and has obtained a recommendation from the Quarterly Conference of which he is a member, certifying his qualifications in doctrine, discipline, talents, and usefulness, signed by the President, and countersigned by the Secretary. He shall, if he cannot attend, send to the Annual

Conference such recommendation, and a note certifying his belief in the doctrine and discipline of our Church. The whole being examined by the Annual Conference, and if approved he may be ordained.

3. Every Local Elder, Deacon, or Preacher shall be amenable to the Quarterly Conference where he resides, for his Christian character and the faithful performance of his ministerial office. He shall have his name recorded on the journal of said Conference, and also enrolled on a class paper, and shall meet in class; and in neglect of the above duties, the Quarterly Conference, if they judge it proper, may deprive him of his ministerial office. And when a preacher is located, or discontinued by an Annual Conference, he shall be amenable to the Quarterly Conference of the circuit or station where he had his last appointment, or at the place where he shall reside at the time of his location.

4. Whenever any Elder, Deacon, or Preacher shall remove from one circuit or station to another, he shall procure from the Presiding Elder of the district, or from the preacher having charge, a certificate of his official standing in the Church at the time of his removal, without which he shall

not be received as a Local Preacher in other places.

5. The Presiding Elders and the Preachers in charge are required so to arrange the appointments, wherever it is practicable, as to give the Local Preachers regular and systematic employment on the Sabbath.

SECTION III.

The Trial of Local Preachers.

Quest. 1. What shall be done when a Local Elder, Deacon, or Preacher is reported to be guilty of some crime expressly forbidden in the word of God, sufficient to exclude a person from the kingdom of grace and glory?

Answ. 1. The Preacher having charge shall call a committee, consisting of three or more Local Preachers, before whom it shall be the duty of the accused to appear, and by whom he shall he acquitted, or, if found guilty, suspended until the next Quarterly Conference. And the Preacher in charge shall cause exact minutes of the charges, testimony, and examination, together with the decision of the committee, to be laid before the Quarterly Conference, where it shall be the duty of the accused to appear. If the accused refuse or neglect to appear before said committee, he may be tried in his absence.

And the President shall, at the commencement of the trial, appoint a Secretary, who shall take down regular minutes of the evidence of the trial; which minutes, when read and approved, shall be signed by the President, and also by the members of the Conference who are present, or a majority of them. And in case of condemnation, the Local Preacher, Deacon, or Elder shall be allowed to appeal to the next Annual Conference, provided that he signify to the said Quarterly Conference his determination to appeal; in which case the said President shall lay the minutes of the trial above mentioned before the said Annual Conference, at which the Local Preacher, Deacon, or Elder, so appealing, may appear: and the said Annual Conference by committee, as in the case of accused Traveling Preachers, or in full session, shall judge, and finally determine from the minutes of the said trial, so laid before them.

2. When a Local Elder, or Deacon, shall be expelled, the Presiding Elder shall require of him the credentials of his ordina-

tion, to be filed with the papers of the Annual Conference within the limits of which the expulsion has taken place. And should he, at any future time, produce to the Annual Conference a certificate of his restoration, signed by the President, and countersigned by the Secretary of the Quarterly Conference, his credentials may be restored to him.

Quest. 2. What shall be done in cases of improper tempers, words, or actions?

Answ. The person so offending shall be reprehended by the Preacher having charge. Should a second transgression take place, one, two, or three faithful friends are to be taken as witnesses. If he be not then cured, he shall be tried at the next Quarterly Conference, and if found guilty and impenitent, he shall be expelled from the Church.

Quest. 3. What shall be done when a Local Elder, Deacon, or Preacher fails in business, or contracts debts which he is not able to pay?

Answ. Let the Preacher in charge appoint three judicious members of the Church to inspect the accounts, contracts, and circumstances of the supposed delinquent; and if, in their opinion, he has behaved dishonestly, or contracted debts without the probability of paying, let the case be disposed of according to the answer to question one of this section.

SECTION IV.

Local Preachers to have an Allowance in certain Cases.

1. Whenever a Local Preacher fills the place of a Traveling Preacher by the approbation of the Presiding Elder, he shall be paid for his time a sum proportional to the allowance of a Traveling Preacher; which sum shall be paid by the circuit at the next quarterly meeting, if the Traveling Preacher whose place he filled up were either sick or necessarily absent; or, in other cases, out of the allowance of the Traveling Preacher.

2. If a Local Preacher be distressed in his temporal circumstances on account of his service in the circuit, he may apply to the Quarterly Conference, who may give him what relief they judge proper, after the allowance of the Traveling Preachers and of their wives, and all other regular allowances, are discharged.

SECTION V.

The Rights and Privileges of Preachers and Official Members of our Colored Membership.

1. Our Colored Preachers and official members shall have all the privileges which are usual to others in Quarterly Conferences, where the usages of the country do not forbid it. And the Presiding Elder may hold for them a separate Quarterly Conference, when in his judgment it shall be expedient.

2. The Bishop or Presiding Elder may employ Colored Preachers to travel and preach, when their services are judged necessary. *Provided*, that no one shall be so employed without having been recommended by a Quarterly Conference.

3. The Bishops may call a Conference once in each year of our Colored Local Preachers, within the bounds of any one or more of our districts, for the purpose of conferring with them with respect to the wants of the work among our colored people, and the best means to be employed in promoting its prosperity; at which Conference, the Presiding Elder within whose district, and under whose care, the colored Churches and congregations are, shall be

present. *Provided*, that the holding of said Conference or Conferences shall be recommended by an Annual Conference, and the Bishops, upon due inquiry, shall deem it practicable and expedient.

CHAPTER IX.

OF STEWARDS.

Qualifications, Appointment, and Duties of Stewards.

Quest. 1. What are the qualifications necessary for Stewards?

Answ. Let them be men of solid piety, who both know and love the Methodist doctrine and discipline, and of good natural and acquired abilities to transact the temporal business.

Quest. 2. How are the Stewards to be appointed?

Answ. The preacher having the charge of the circuit shall have the right of nomination; but the Quarterly Conference shall confirm or reject such nomination. The Stewards so appointed shall hold office for one year, but may be reappointed in like manner from year to year.

Quest. 3. What are the duties of Stewards?

Answ. To take an exact account of all the money or other provisions collected for the support of Preachers in the circuit or station, and apply the same as the Discipline directs; to make an accurate return of every expenditure of money, whether to the preachers, the sick, or the poor; to seek the needy and distressed in order to relieve and comfort them; to inform the Preachers of any sick or disorderly persons; to tell the preachers what they think wrong in them; to attend the quarterly meetings of their circuit, and leaders' meetings; to give advice, if asked, in planning the circuit; to attend committees for the application of money to Churches; to give counsel in matters of arbitration; provide elements for the Lord's Supper; to write circular letters to the societies in the circuit to be more liberal if need be; as also to let them know, when occasion requires, the state of the temporal concerns at the last quarterly meeting; to register the marriages and baptisms; and to be subject to the Bishops, the Presiding Elder of their district, and the Elder, Deacon, and Traveling Preachers of their circuit.

Quest. 4. To whom are Stewards accountable for the faithful performance of their duty?

Answ. To the Quarterly Conference of the circuit or station, which shall have power to dismiss or change them at pleasure.

Quest. 5. What number of Stewards are necessary in each circuit?

Answ. Not less than three, nor more than nine, one of whom shall be the Recording Steward.

CHAPTER X.

THE MEMBERSHIP OF THE CHURCH.

SECTION I.

Of Receiving Members into the Church.

Quest. 1. How shall we prevent improper persons from insinuating themselves into the Church?

Answ. 1. *Let none be received into the Church until they are recommended by a leader with whom they have met at least six months on trial, and have been baptized; and shall on examination by the minister in charge, before the Church, give satisfactory assurances both of the correctness of their faith, and their willingness to observe and keep the rules of the Church.* Nevertheless, if a member in good standing in any other orthodox Church shall desire to unite with us, such applicant may, by giving satisfactory answers to the usual inquiries, be received at once into full fellowship.

2. Let none be admitted on trial, except they are well recommended by one you know, or until they have met twice or thrice in class.

3. Read the rules to them the first time they meet.

Quest. 2. How shall we be more exact in receiving and excluding members?

Answ. The official minister or preacher shall, at every quarterly meeting, read the names of those that are received into the Church, and also those that are excluded therefrom.

SECTION II.

How an accused Member is to be brought to trial.

I. FOR IMMORAL CONDUCT.

Quest. 1. How shall an accused member be brought to trial?

Answ. Before the society of which he is a member, or a select number, who shall not be members of the Quarterly Conference, (and if the preacher judge necessary, the Committee may be selected from any charge within the district,) in the presence of the Preacher in charge, who shall preside in the trial, and cause exact minutes of the evidence and proceedings in the case to be taken. In case of trial before a select number, the parties may challenge for cause. If the accused person be found guilty by the decision of a majority of the members before whom he is brought to trial, and the crime be such as is expressly forbidden by the word of God, sufficient to exclude a person from the kingdom of grace and glory, let the Minister or Preacher who has the charge of the circuit expel him. If the accused person evade a trial, by absenting himself, after sufficient notice given him, and the circumstances of the accusation afford strong presumption of guilt, let him be esteemed as guilty, and be accordingly excluded. Witnesses from without shall not be rejected.

II. FOR NEGLECT OF DUTY, OR IMPRUDENT CONDUCT.

But in cases of neglect of duties of any kind, imprudent conduct, indulging sinful tempers or words, the buying, selling, or using intoxicating liquors as a beverage, or disobedience to the order and discipline of the Church: First, let private reproof be given by a Preacher or leader; and if there be an acknowledgment of the fault, and proper humiliation, the person may be borne with. On a second offense, the Preacher or leader may take one or two faithful friends. On a third offense, let the case be brought before the society, or a select number; and if there be no sign of real humiliation, the offender must be cut off.

III. FOR DISSENSION.

1. If a member of our Church shall be clearly convicted of endeavoring to sow dissensions in any of our societies, by inveighing against either our doctrines or discipline, such person so offending shall be first reproved by the senior Minister or Preacher of his circuit, and if he persist in such pernicious practices, he shall be expelled from the Church.

2. *Nevertheless*, if in any of the above-mentioned cases the Minister or Preacher differ in judgment from the majority of the society, or the select number, concerning the innocence or guilt of the accused person, the trial, in such case, may be referred by the Minister or Preacher to the ensuing Quarterly Conference, which shall have authority to order a new trial.

3. If there be a murmur or complaint from any excluded person, in any of the above-mentioned instances, that justice has not been done, he shall be allowed an appeal to the next Quarterly Conference: except such as absent themselves from

trial, after sufficient notice is given them; and the Preacher in charge shall present exact minutes of the evidence and proceedings of the trial to the Quarterly Conference, from which minutes the case shall finally be determined.

4. After such forms of trial and expulsion, such person shall have no privileges of society or of sacraments in our Church, without contrition, confession, and satisfactory reformation.

IV. RULES FOR THE SETTLEMENT OF DISPUTED DEBTS, AND ARBITRATION THEREON.

Quest. 2. How shall disputes between members of our Church concerning the payment of debts or otherwise be settled?

Answ. 1. On any dispute between two or more of the members of our Church, concerning the payment of debts, or otherwise, which cannot be settled by the parties concerned, the Preacher who has the charge of the circuit shall inquire into the circumstances of the case; and shall recommend to the contending parties a reference, consisting of one arbiter chosen by the plaintiff, and another chosen by the defendant; which two arbiters so chosen shall nominate the third; the three arbiters being members of our Church.

Answ. 2. But if one of these parties be dissatisfied with the judgment given, such party may apply to the ensuing Quarterly Conference of the circuit for allowance to have a *second* arbitration appointed; and if the Quarterly Conference see sufficient reason, they shall grant a *second* arbitration, in which case each party shall choose two arbiters, and the four arbiters shall choose a fifth, the judgment of the majority of whom shall be final; and any person refusing to abide by such judgment shall be excluded the Church.

Answ. 3. And if any member of our Church shall refuse, in cases of debt or other disputes, to refer the matter to arbitration, when recommended by him who has the charge of the circuit, or shall enter into a lawsuit with another member before these measures are taken, he shall be expelled, unless the case be of such a nature as to require and justify a process at law.

V. RULES TO BE OBSERVED TOWARD A MEMBER WHO REFUSES TO PAY HIS DEBTS.

1. Whenever a complaint is made against any member of our Church for non-pay-

ment of debt, when the accounts are adjusted, and the amount ascertained, the Preacher having the charge shall call the debtor before a committee of at least three, to show cause why he does not make payment. The committee shall determine what further time shall be granted him for payment; and what security, if any, shall be given for payment; and in case the debtor refuses to comply, he shall be expelled; but in such case he may appeal to the Quarterly Conference, and their decision shall be final. And in case the creditor complains that justice is not done him, he may lay his grievance before the Quarterly Conference, and their decision shall be final; and if the creditor refuse to comply, he shall be expelled.

VI. RULES CONCERNING INSOLVENCY ON THE PART OF ANY OF OUR MEMBERS.

Quest. 3. What shall be done in case of insolvency on the part of any of our members?

Answ. 1. The Preachers who have the oversight of circuits are required to execute all our rules fully and strenuously against all frauds, and particularly against dishonest insolvencies; suffering none to remain in our Church on any account who are found guilty of any fraud.

2. To prevent scandal, when any of our members fail in business, or contract debts which they are not able to pay, let two or three judicious members of the Church inspect the accounts, contracts, and circumstances of the case of the supposed delinquent; and if they judge that he has behaved dishonestly, or borrowed money without a probability of paying, let him be brought to trial, and if found guilty, expelled.

PART III.

THE RITUAL.

I.

The Ritual of Baptism.

1. Let every adult person, and the parents of every child to be baptized, have the choice either of immersion, sprinkling, or pouring.

2. We will on no account whatever make a charge for administering baptism, or for burying the dead.

I. The Ministration of Baptism to Children.

The minister coming to the font, which is to be filled with pure water, shall use the following.

Dearly beloved, forasmuch as all men are conceived and born in sin, and that our Saviour Christ saith none can enter into the kingdom of God, except he be regenerate and born anew of water and of the Holy Ghost; I beseech you to call upon God the Father, through our Lord Jesus Christ, that of his bounteous mercy he will grant to *this child* that thing which by nature *he* cannot have, that *he* may be baptized with water and the Holy Ghost, and received into Christ's holy Church, and be made a *lively member* of the same.

Then shall the minister say,

Let us pray.

Almighty and everlasting God, who of thy great mercy didst save Noah and his family in the ark from perishing by water; and also didst safely lead the children of Israel, thy people, through the Red Sea, figuring thereby thy holy baptism; and by the baptism of thy well-beloved Son Jesus Christ, in the river Jordan, didst sanctify water for this holy sacrament: we beseech thee, for thine infinite mercies, that thou wilt look upon *this child:* wash *him* and sanctify *him* with the Holy Ghost; that *he*, being delivered from thy wrath, may be received into the ark of Christ's Church, and being steadfast in faith, joyful through hope, and rooted in love, may so pass the waves of this troublesome world, that finally *he* may come to the land of everlasting life; there to reign with thee, world without end, through Jesus Christ our Lord. *Amen.*

O merciful God, grant that the old Adam in *this child* may be so buried, that the new man may be raised up in *him*. *Amen.*

Grant that all carnal affections may die in *him*, and that all things belonging to the Spirit may live and grow in *him*. *Amen.*

Grant that *he* may have power and strength to have victory, and to triumph against the devil, the world, and the flesh. *Amen.*

Grant that whosoever is dedicated to thee by our office and ministry may also be endued with heavenly virtues, and everlastingly rewarded through thy mercy, O blessed Lord God, who dost live and govern all things, world without end. *Amen.*

Almighty, ever-living God, whose most dearly beloved Son Jesus Christ, for the forgiveness of our sins, did shed out of his most precious side both water and blood, and gave commandment to his disciples that they should go teach all nations, and baptize them in the name of the Father, and of the Son, and of the Holy Ghost; regard, we beseech thee, the supplications of thy congregation; sanctify this water for this holy sacrament; and grant that *this child* now to be baptized may receive the fullness of thy grace, and ever remain in the number of thy faithful and elect children, through Jesus Christ our Lord. *Amen.*

Then shall the people stand up, and the minister shall say,

Hear the words of the Gospel written by St. Mark, in the tenth chapter, at the thirteenth verse.

They brought young children to Christ, that he should touch them. And his disciples rebuked those that brought them; but when Jesus saw it, he was much displeased, and said unto them, Suffer the little children to come unto me, and forbid them not, for of such is the kingdom of God. Verily I say unto you, Whosoever shall not receive the kingdom of God as a little child, he shall not enter therein. And he took them up in his arms, put his hands upon them, and blessed them.

Then the minister shall take the child into his hands, and say to the friends of the child,

Name this child.

And then, naming it after them, he shall sprinkle or pour water upon it, or, if desired, immerse it in water, saying,

N., I baptize thee in the name of the Father, and of the Son, and of the Holy Ghost. *Amen.*

Then shall be said, all kneeling,

Our Father who art in heaven, hallowed be thy name; thy kingdom come; thy will be done on earth as it is in heaven: give us this day our daily bread; and forgive us our trespasses, as we forgive them that trespass against us; and lead us not into temptation, but deliver us from evil. *Amen.*

Then shall the minister conclude with extemporary prayer.

II. The Ministration of Baptism to such as are of Riper Years.

Dearly beloved, forasmuch as all men are conceived and born in sin, (and that which is born of the flesh is flesh, and they that are in the flesh cannot please God, but live in sin, committing many actual transgressions,) and that our Saviour Christ saith, None can enter into the kingdom of God, except he be regenerate and born anew of water and of the Holy Ghost; I beseech you to call upon God the Father, through our Lord Jesus Christ, that of his bounteous goodness he will grant to *these persons* that which by nature *they* cannot have; that *they* may be baptized with water and the Holy Ghost, and received into Christ's holy Church, and be made lively *members* of the same.

Then shall the minister say,

Almighty and immortal God, the aid of all that need, the helper of all that flee to thee for succor, the life of them that believe, and the resurrection of the dead; we call upon thee for *these persons*, that *they*, coming to thy holy baptism, may receive remission of *their sins*, by spiritual regeneration. Receive *them*, O Lord, as thou hast promised by thy well-beloved Son, saying, Ask, and ye shall receive; seek, and ye shall find; knock, and it shall be opened unto you: so give now unto us that ask; let us that seek, find; open the gate unto us that knock; that *these persons* may enjoy the everlasting benediction of thy heavenly washing, and may come to the eternal kingdom which thou hast promised by Christ our Lord. *Amen.*

After which he shall say,

Almighty and everlasting God, heavenly Father, we give thee humble thanks, for that thou hast vouchsafed to call us to the knowledge of thy grace, and faith in thee; increase this knowledge and confirm this faith in us evermore. Give thy Holy Spirit to *these persons*, that *they* may be born again, and be made *heirs* of everlasting salvation through our Lord Jesus Christ, who liveth and reigneth with thee and the Holy Spirit, now and forever. *Amen.*

Then shall the people stand up, and the minister shall say,

Hear the words of the Gospel written by St. John, in the third chapter, beginning at the first verse.

There was a man of the Pharisees, named Nicodemus, a ruler of the Jews: the same came to Jesus by night, and said unto him, Rabbi, we know that thou art a teacher come from God: for no man can do these miracles that thou doest, except God be with him. Jesus answered and said unto him, Verily, verily, I say unto thee, Except a man be born again, he cannot see the kingdom of God. Nicodemus saith unto him, How can a man be born when he is old? Can he enter the second time into his mother's womb, and be born? Jesus answered, Verily, verily, I say unto thee, Except a man be born of water, and of the Spirit, he cannot enter into the kingdom of God. That which is born of the flesh is flesh; and that which is born of the Spirit is spirit. Marvel not that I said unto thee, Ye must be born again. The wind bloweth where it listeth, and thou hearest the sound thereof, but canst not tell whence it cometh, and whither it goeth: so is every one that is born of the Spirit.

Then the minister shall speak to the persons *to be baptized on this wise:*

Well beloved, who *are* come hither, desiring to receive holy baptism, *ye* have heard how the congregation hath prayed that our Lord Jesus Christ would vouchsafe to receive you, and bless you, to release you of your sins, to give you the kingdom of heaven, and everlasting life. And our Lord Jesus Christ hath promised in his holy word to grant all those things that we have prayed for: which promise he for his part will most surely keep and perform.

Wherefore after this promise made by Christ, *you* must also faithfully, for *your* part, promise, in the presence of this whole congregation, that you will renounce the devil and all his works, and constantly believe God's holy word, and obediently keep his commandments.

Then shall the minister demand of each of the persons to be baptized, severally,

Quest. Dost thou renounce the devil and all his works, the vain pomp and glory of the world, with all covetous desires of the same, and the carnal desires of the flesh, so that thou wilt not follow or be led by them?

Answ. I renounce them all.

Quest. Dost thou believe in God the Father Almighty, Maker of heaven and earth? and in Jesus Christ his only-begotten Son our Lord? and that he was conceived by the Holy Ghost, born of the Virgin Mary? that he suffered under Pontius Pilate, was crucified, dead, and buried; that he rose again the third day; that he ascended into heaven, and sitteth at the right hand of God the Father Almighty, and from thence shall come again, at the end of the world, to judge the quick and the dead?

And dost thou believe in the Holy Ghost, the holy catholic Church,* the communion of saints, the remission of sins, the resurrection of the body, and everlasting life after death?

Answ. All this I steadfastly believe.

Quest. Wilt thou be baptized in this faith?

Answ. This is my desire.

Quest. Wilt thou then obediently keep God's holy will and commandments, and walk in the same all the days of thy life?

Answ. I will endeavor so to do, God being my helper.

* By the holy catholic Church is meant the Church of God in general.

Then shall the minister say,

O merciful God, grant that the old Adam in *these persons* may be so buried, that the new man may be raised up in *them*. *Amen.*

Grant that all carnal affections may die in *them*, and that all things belonging to the Spirit may live and grow in *them*. *Amen.*

Grant that *they* may have power and strength to have victory, and triumph against the devil, the world, and the flesh. *Amen.*

Grant that *they* being here dedicated to thee by our office and ministry, may also be endued with heavenly virtues, and everlastingly rewarded, through thy mercy, O blessed Lord God, who dost live and govern all things, world without end. *Amen.*

Almighty, ever-living God, whose most dearly beloved Son Jesus Christ, for the forgiveness of our sins, did shed out of his most precious side both water and blood; and gave commandment to his disciples that they should go teach all nations, and baptize them in the name of the Father, and of the Son, and of the Holy Ghost; regard, we beseech thee, the supplications of this congregation, and grant that the

10

persons now to be baptized may receive the fullness of thy grace, and ever remain in the number of thy faithful and elect children, through Jesus Christ our Lord. *Amen.*

Then shall the minister take each person to be baptized by the right hand: and placing him conveniently by the font, according to his discretion, shall ask the name; and then shall sprinkle or pour water upon him, (or, if he shall desire it, shall immerse him in water,) saying,

N., I baptize thee in the name of the Father, and of the Son, and of the Holy Ghost. *Amen.*

Then shall be said the Lord's Prayer, all kneeling.

Our Father who art in heaven, hallowed be thy name; thy kingdom come; thy will be done on earth, as it is in heaven; give us this day our daily bread; and forgive us our trespasses, as we forgive them that trespass against us; and lead us not into temptation, but deliver us from evil. *Amen.*

[*Then let the minister conclude with extemporary prayer.*]

II.

The Lord's Supper.

Quest. Are there any directions to be given concerning the administration of the Lord's Supper?

Answ. 1. Let those who have scruples concerning the receiving of it kneeling, be permitted to receive it either standing or sitting.

2. No person shall be admitted to the Lord's Supper among us who is guilty of any practice for which we would exclude a member of our Church.

ORDER FOR THE ADMINISTRATION OF THE LORD'S SUPPER.

The Elder shall say one or more of these sentences:

LET your light so shine before men, that they may see your good works, and glorify your Father which is in heaven. Matt. v, 16.

Lay not up for yourselves treasures upon earth, where moth and rust doth corrupt, and where thieves break through and steal; but lay up for yourselves treasures in heaven, where neither moth nor rust doth corrupt, and where thieves do not break through nor steal. Matt. vi, 19, 20.

Whatsoever ye would that men should

do to you, do ye even so to them: for this is the law and the prophets. Matt. vii, 12.

Not every one that saith unto me, Lord, Lord, shall enter into the kingdom of heaven; but he that doeth the will of my Father which is in heaven. Matt. vii, 21.

Zaccheus stood, and said unto the Lord, Behold, Lord, the half of my goods I give to the poor; and if I have taken anything from any man by false accusation, I restore him fourfold. Luke xix, 8.

He which soweth sparingly shall reap also sparingly; and he which soweth bountifully shall reap also bountifully. Every man according as he purposeth in his heart, so let him give; not grudgingly, or of necessity: for God loveth a cheerful giver. 2 Cor. ix, 6, 7.

As we have therefore opportunity, let us do good unto all men, especially unto them who are of the household of faith. Gal. vi, 10.

Godliness with contentment is great gain; for we brought nothing into this world, and it is certain we can carry nothing out. 1 Tim. vi, 6, 7.

Charge them that are rich in this world, that they be ready to distribute, willing to communicate, laying up in store for themselves a good foundation against the time to come, that they may lay hold on eternal life. 1 Tim. vi, 17–19.

God is not unrighteous to forget your work and labor of love, which ye have showed toward his name, in that ye have ministered to the saints, and do minister. Heb. vi, 10.

To do good, and to communicate, forget not; for with such sacrifices God is well pleased. Heb. xiii, 16.

Whoso hath this world's good, and seeth his brother have need, and shutteth up his bowels of compassion from him, how dwelleth the love of God in him? 1 John iii, 17.

He that hath pity upon the poor, lendeth unto the Lord; and that which he hath given will he pay him again. Prov. xix, 17.

Blessed is he that considereth the poor: the Lord will deliver him in time of trouble. Psalm xli, 1.

[While these sentences are in reading, some fit person, appointed for that purpose, shall receive the alms for the poor, and other devotions of the people, in a decent basin, to be provided for that purpose; and then bring it to the Elder, who shall place it upon the table.]

After which the Elder shall say,

Ye that do truly and earnestly repent of your sins, and are in love and charity with your neighbors, and intend to lead a new life, following the commandments of God, and walking from henceforth in his holy ways; draw near with faith, and take this holy sacrament to your comfort, and make your humble confession to Almighty God, meekly kneeling upon your knees.

Then shall this general confession be made by the Minister in the name of all those who are minded to receive the holy communion, both he and all the people kneeling humbly upon their knees, and saying,

Almighty God, Father of our Lord Jesus Christ, Maker of all things, Judge of all men; we acknowledge and bewail our manifold sins and wickedness, which we from time to time most grievously have committed, by thought, word, and deed, against thy Divine Majesty, provoking most justly thy wrath and indignation against us. We do earnestly repent, and are heartily sorry for these our misdoings; the remembrance of them is grievous unto us. Have mercy upon us, have mercy upon us, most merciful Father; for thy Son, our Lord Jesus Christ's sake, forgive us all that is past, and grant that we may ever hereafter serve and please thee in newness of life, to the honor and glory of thy name, through Jesus Christ our Lord. *Amen.*

Then shall the Elder say,

O Almighty God, our heavenly Father, who of thy great mercy hast promised forgiveness of sins to all them that with hearty repentance and true faith turn unto thee; have mercy upon us; pardon and deliver us from all our sins, confirm and strengthen us in all goodness, and bring us to everlasting life, through Jesus Christ our Lord. *Amen.*

The Collect.

Almighty God, unto whom all hearts be open, all desires known, and from whom no secrets are hid; cleanse the thoughts of our hearts by the inspiration of thy Holy Spirit, that we may perfectly love thee, and worthily magnify thy holy name, through Christ our Lord. *Amen.*

Then shall the Elder say,

It is very meet, right, and our bounden duty, that we should at all times, and in all places, give thanks unto thee, O Lord, holy Father, almighty, everlasting God.

Therefore with angels and archangels, and with all the company of heaven, we laud and magnify thy glorious name, evermore praising thee, and saying, Holy, holy, holy, Lord God of hosts, heaven and earth are full of thy glory. Glory be to thee, O Lord most high. *Amen.*

Then shall the Elder say,

We do not presume to come to this thy table, O merciful Lord, trusting in our own righteousness, but in thy manifold and great mercies. We are not worthy so much as to gather up the crumbs under thy table. But thou art the same Lord, whose property is always to have mercy: Grant us, therefore, gracious Lord, so to eat the flesh of thy dear Son Jesus Christ, and to drink his blood, that our sinful souls and bodies may be made clean by his death, and washed through his most precious blood, and that we may evermore dwell in him, and he in us. *Amen.*

Then the Elder shall say the prayer of consecration, as followeth:

Almighty God, our heavenly Father, who of thy tender mercy didst give thine only Son Jesus Christ to suffer death upon the cross for our redemption; who made there (by his oblation of himself once offered) a full, perfect, and sufficient sacrifice, oblation, and satisfaction for the sins of the whole world; and did institute, and in his holy Gospel command us to continue, a perpetual memory of that his precious death until his coming again: hear us, O merciful Father, we most humbly beseech thee, and grant that we, receiving these thy creatures of bread and wine, according to thy Son our Saviour Jesus Christ's holy institution, in remembrance of his death and passion, may be partakers of his most blessed body and blood; who in the same night that he was betrayed, took bread; (1) and when he had given thanks, he broke it (2) and gave it to his disciples, saying, Take, eat; this (3) is my body which is given for you; do this in remembrance of me. Likewise after supper he took (4) the cup; and when he had given thanks, he gave it to them, saying,

(1) *Here the Elder is to take the plate of bread into his hand.*

(2) *And here to break the bread.*

(3) *And here to lay his hands upon all the bread.*

(4) *Here he is to take the cup in his hand.*

Drink ye all of this: for this (5) is my blood of the New Testament, which is shed for you and for many, for the remission of sins; do this, as oft as ye shall drink it, in remembrance of me. *Amen.*

(5) *And here to lay his hand upon all the vessels which contain the wine.*

Then shall the Minister first receive the communion in both kinds himself, and then proceed to deliver the same to the other Ministers in like manner, (if any be present,) and after that to the people also, in order, into their hands. And when he delivereth the bread, he shall say,

The body of our Lord Jesus Christ, which was given for *thee*, preserve *thy soul* and *body* unto everlasting life. Take and eat this in remembrance that Christ died for *thee*, and feed on him in *thy heart* by faith with thanksgiving.

And the Minister that delivereth the cup shall say,

The blood of our Lord Jesus Christ, which was shed for *thee*, preserve *thy soul* and *body* unto everlasting life. Drink this in remembrance that Christ's blood was shed for *thee*, and be thankful.

[If the consecrated bread or wine be all spent before all have communicated, the Elder may consecrate more, by repeating the prayer of consecration.]

[When all have communicated, the minister shall return to the Lord's table, and place upon it what remaineth of the consecrated elements, covering the same with a fair linen cloth.]

Then shall the Elder say the Lord's Prayer; the people repeating after him every petition.

Our Father who art in heaven, hallowed be thy name; thy kingdom come; thy will be done on earth, as it is in heaven; give us this day our daily bread; and forgive us our trespasses, as we forgive them that trespass against us; and lead us not into temptation, but deliver us from evil, for thine is the kingdom, and the power, and the glory, for ever and ever. *Amen.*

After which shall be said as followeth:

O Lord and heavenly Father, we thy humble servants desire thy fatherly goodness mercifully to accept this our sacrifice of praise and thanksgiving; most humbly beseeching thee to grant that, by the merits and death of thy Son Jesus Christ, and through faith in his blood, we and thy whole Church may obtain remission of our sins, and all other benefits of his passion. And here we offer and present unto thee, O Lord, ourselves, our souls and bodies, to be a reasonable, holy, and lively sacrifice unto thee; humbly beseeching thee that all we who are partakers of this holy communion may be filled with thy grace and heavenly benediction. And although we be unworthy, through our manifold sins, to offer unto thee any sacrifice, yet we beseech thee to accept this our bounden duty and service; not weighing our merits, but pardoning our offenses, through Jesus Christ our Lord: by whom, and with whom, in the unity of the Holy Ghost, all honor and glory be unto thee, O Father Almighty, world without end. *Amen.*

Then shall be said,

Glory be to God on high, and on earth peace, good-will toward men. We praise thee, we bless thee, we worship thee, we glorify thee, we give thanks to thee for thy great glory, O Lord God, heavenly King, God the Father Almighty.

O Lord, the only-begotten Son Jesus Christ; O Lord God, Lamb of God, Son of the Father, that takest away the sins of the world, have mercy upon us. Thou that takest away the sins of the world, have mercy upon us. Thou that takest away the sins of the world, receive our prayer. Thou that sittest at the right hand of God the Father, have mercy upon us.

For thou only art holy; thou only art the Lord; thou only, O Christ, with the Holy Ghost, art most high in the glory of God the Father. *Amen.*

Then the Elder, if he see it expedient, may put up an extemporary prayer; and afterward shall let the people depart with this blessing:

May the peace of God, which passeth all understanding, keep your hearts and minds in the knowledge and love of God, and of his Son Jesus Christ our Lord; and the blessing of God Almighty, the Father, the Son, and the Holy Ghost, be among you, and remain with you always. *Amen.*

N. B. If the Elder be straitened for time, he may omit any part of the service except the prayer of consecration.

III.

Form of Solemnization of Matrimony.

First, the bans of all that are to be married together must be published in the congregation three several Sundays in the time of Divine service, (unless they be otherwise qualified according to law,) the Minister saying after the accustomed manner,

I PUBLISH the bans of marriage between M. of ——, and N. of ——. If any of you know cause or just impediment why these two persons should not be joined together in holy matrimony, *ye* are to declare it. This is the first [*second or third*] time of asking.

At the day and time appointed for solemnization of matrimony, the persons to be married standing together, the man on the right hand, and the woman on the left, the Minister shall say,

Dearly beloved, we are gathered together here in the sight of God, and in the presence of these witnesses, to join together this man and this woman in holy matrimony: which is an honorable estate, instituted of God in the time of man's innocency, signifying unto us the mystical union that is between Christ and his Church; which holy estate Christ adorned and beautified with his presence, and first miracle that he wrought in Cana of Galilee, and is commended of St. Paul to be honorable among all men: and therefore is not by any to be enterprised, or taken in hand unadvisedly, but reverently, discreetly, advisedly, and in the fear of God.

Into which holy estate these two persons present come now to be joined. Therefore, if any can show any just cause why they may not lawfully be joined together, let him now speak, or else hereafter forever hold his peace.

And also speaking unto the persons that are to be married, he shall say,

I require and charge you both, (as you will answer at the dreadful day of judgment, when the secrets of all hearts shall be disclosed,) that if either of you know any impediment why you may not be lawfully joined together in matrimony, you do now confess it: for be ye well assured, that so many as are coupled together otherwise than God's word doth allow, are not joined together by God, neither is their matrimony lawful.

If no impediment be alleged, then shall the minister say unto the man,

M., Wilt thou have this woman to thy wedded wife, to live together after God's ordinance, in the holy estate of matrimony? Wilt thou love her, comfort her, honor, and keep her, in sickness and in health; and, forsaking all other, keep thee only unto her, so long as ye both shall live?

The man shall answer,

I will.

Then shall the minister say unto the woman,

N., Wilt thou have this man to thy wedded husband, to live together after God's ordinance, in the holy estate of matrimony? Wilt thou obey him, serve him, love, honor, and keep him, in sickness and in health; and, forsaking all other, keep thee only unto him, so long as ye both shall live?

The woman shall answer,

I will.

Then the minister shall cause the man with his right hand to take the woman by her right hand, and to say after him as followeth:

I, *M.*, take thee, *N.*, to be my wedded wife, to have and to hold, from this day forward, for better, for worse, for richer, for poorer, in sickness and in health, to love, and to cherish, till death us do part, according to God's holy ordinance: and thereto I plight thee my faith.

Then shall they loose their hands, and the woman with her right hand taking the man by his right hand, shall likewise say after the minister:

I, *N.*, take thee, *M.*, to be my wedded husband, to have and to hold, from this day forward, for better, for worse, for richer, for poorer, in sickness and in health, to love, cherish, and to obey, till death us do part, according to God's holy ordinance: and thereto I give thee my faith.

Then shall the minister say,

Let us pray.

O eternal God, Creator and Preserver of all mankind, Giver of all spiritual grace, the Author of everlasting life; send thy blessing upon these thy servants, this man and this woman, whom we bless in thy name; that as Isaac and Rebecca lived faithfully together, so these persons may surely perform and keep the vow and covenant between them made, and may ever remain in perfect love and peace together, and live according to thy laws, through Jesus Christ our Lord. *Amen.*

Then shall the minister join their right hands together, and say,

Those whom God hath joined together let no man put asunder.

Forasmuch as *M.* and *N.* have consented together in holy wedlock, and have witnessed the same before God and this company, and thereto have pledged their faith either to other, and have declared the same by joining of hands, I pronounce that they are man and wife together, in the name of the Father, and of the Son, and of the Holy Ghost. *Amen.*

And the minister shall add this blessing:

God the Father, God the Son, God the Holy Ghost, bless, preserve, and keep you; the Lord mercifully with his favor look upon you, and so fill you with all spiritual benediction and grace, that ye may so live together in this life, that in the world to come ye may have life everlasting. *Amen.*

Then the minister shall say,

Our Father who art in heaven, hallowed be thy name; thy kingdom come; thy will be done on earth, as it is in heaven; give us this day our daily bread; and forgive us our trespasses, as we forgive them that trespass against us; and lead us not into temptation, but deliver us from evil. *Amen.*

Then shall the minister say,

O God of Abraham, God of Isaac, God of Jacob, bless this man and this woman, and sow the seed of eternal life in their hearts, that whatsoever in thy holy word they shall profitably learn, they may indeed fulfill the same. Look, O Lord, mercifully on them from heaven, and bless them; and as thou didst send thy blessings upon Abraham and Sarah, to their great comfort, so vouchsafe to send thy blessings upon this man and this woman, that they, obeying thy will, and always being in safety under thy protection, may abide in thy love unto their lives' end, through Jesus Christ our Lord. *Amen.*

O God, who by thy mighty power hast made all things of nothing; who also (after other things set in order) didst appoint that out of man (created after thine own image and similitude) woman should take her beginning; and knitting them together, didst teach that it should never be lawful to put asunder those whom thou, by matrimony, hadst made one: O God, who hast consecrated the state of matrimony to such an excellent mystery, that in it is signified and represented the spiritual marriage and unity between Christ and his Church; look mercifully upon this man and this woman; that this man may love his wife, according to thy word, (as Christ did love his spouse, the Church, who gave himself for it; loving and cherishing it, even as his own flesh,) and also that this woman may be loving and amiable, faithful and obedient to her husband, and in all quietness, sobriety, and peace, be a follower of holy and godly matrons. O Lord, bless them both, and grant them to inherit thy everlasting kingdom, through Jesus Christ our Lord. *Amen.*

Then shall the minister say,

Almighty God, who at the beginning did create our first parents, Adam and Eve, and did sanctify and join them together in marriage, pour upon you the riches of his grace, sanctify and bless you, that ye may please him both in body and soul, and live together in holy love unto your lives' end. *Amen.*

IV.

Order of the Burial of the Dead.

The minister, meeting the corpse, and going before it, shall say,

I AM the resurrection and the life: he that believeth in me, though he were dead, yet shall he live; and whosoever liveth and believeth in me, shall never die. John xi, 25, 26.

I know that my Redeemer liveth, and that he shall stand at the latter day upon the earth: and though after my skin worms destroy this body, yet in my flesh shall I see God; whom I shall see for myself, and mine eyes shall behold, and not another. Job xix, 25–27.

We brought nothing into this world, and it is certain we can carry nothing out. The Lord gave, and the Lord hath taken away; blessed be the name of the Lord. 1 Tim. vi, 7; Job i, 21.

At the grave, when the corpse is laid in the earth, the minister shall say,

Man that is born of a woman hath but a short time to live, and is full of misery. He cometh up and is cut down like a flower: he fleeth as it were a shadow, and never continueth in one stay.

In the midst of life we are in death: of whom may we seek for succor, but of thee, O Lord, who for our sins art justly displeased?

Yet, O Lord God, most holy, O Lord most mighty, O holy and most merciful Saviour, deliver us not into the bitter pains of eternal death.

Thou knowest, Lord, the secrets of our hearts: shut not thy merciful ears to our prayers, but spare us, Lord most holy, O God most mighty, O holy and merciful Saviour, thou most worthy Judge eternal, suffer us not at our last hour for any pains of death to fall from thee.

Then shall be said,

I heard a voice from heaven saying unto me, Write; from henceforth blessed are the dead who die in the Lord: even so, saith the Spirit; for they rest from their labors.

Then shall the minister say,

Lord, have mercy upon us.
Christ, have mercy upon us.
Lord, have mercy upon us.

Our Father who art in heaven, hallowed be thy name; thy kingdom come; thy will be done on earth, as it is in heaven; give us this day our daily bread; and forgive us our trespasses, as we forgive them that trespass against us; and lead us not into temptation, but deliver us from evil. *Amen.*

The Collect.

O merciful God, the Father of our Lord Jesus Christ, who is the resurrection and the life; in whom whosoever believeth shall live, though he die; and whosoever liveth and believeth in him, shall not die eternally: We meekly beseech thee, O Father, to raise us from the death of sin unto the life of righteousness; that when we shall depart this life we may rest in him; and at the general resurrection on the last day may be found acceptable in thy sight, and receive that blessing which thy well-beloved Son shall then pronounce to all that love and fear thee, saying, Come, ye blessed children of my Father, receive the kingdom prepared for you from the beginning of the world. Grant this, we beseech thee, O merciful Father, through Jesus Christ our Mediator and Redeemer. *Amen.*

The grace of our Lord Jesus Christ, and the love of God, and the fellowship of the Holy Ghost, be with us all evermore. *Amen.*

V.

Forms of Ordination.

I. The Form of Ordaining a Bishop.

The Collect.

Almighty God, who by thy Son Jesus Christ didst give to thy holy apostles many excellent gifts, and didst charge them to feed thy flock; give grace, we beseech thee, to all the ministers and pastors of thy Church, that they may diligently preach thy word and duly administer the godly discipline thereof; and grant to the people that they may obediently follow the same; that all may receive the crown of everlasting glory, through Jesus Christ our Lord. *Amen.*

Then shall be read by one of the Elders,

The Epistle. Acts xx, 17–35.

From Miletus Paul sent to Ephesus, and called the Elders of the Church. And when they were come to him, he said unto them, Ye know, from the first day that I came into Asia, after what manner I have been with you at all seasons, serving the Lord with all humility of mind, and with many tears and temptations which befell me by the lying in wait of the Jews; and how I kept back nothing that was profitable unto you, but have showed you, and have taught you publicly and from house to house, testifying both to the Jews and also to the Greeks, repentance toward God, and faith toward our Lord Jesus Christ. And now behold, I go bound in the Spirit unto Jerusalem, not knowing the things that shall befall me there; save that the Holy Ghost witnesseth in every city, saying that bonds and afflictions abide me. But none of these things move me, neither count I my life dear unto myself, so that I might finish my course with joy, and the ministry which I have received of the Lord Jesus to testify the gospel of the grace of God. And now, behold, I know that ye all, among whom I have gone preaching the kingdom of God, shall see my face no more. Wherefore I take you to record this day, that I am pure from the blood of all men; for I have not shunned to declare unto you all the counsel of God. Take heed therefore unto yourselves, and to all the flock, over the which the Holy Ghost hath made you overseers, to feed the Church of God which he hath purchased with his own blood. For I know this, that after my departing shall grievous wolves enter in among you, not sparing the flock. Also of your own selves shall men arise, speaking perverse things, to draw away disciples after them. Therefore watch, and remember, that by the space of three years I ceased not to warn every one night and day with tears. And now, brethren, I commend you to God, and to the word of his grace, which is able to build you up, and to give you an inheritance among all them which are sanctified. I have coveted no man's silver, or gold, or apparel. Yea, ye yourselves know that these hands have ministered unto my necessities, and to them that were with me. I have showed you all things, how that so laboring ye ought to support the weak, and to remember the words of the Lord Jesus, how he said, It is more blessed to give than to receive.

Then another shall read

The Gospel. St. John, xxi, 15-17.

Jesus saith to Simon Peter, Simon, son of Jonas, lovest thou me more than these?

He saith unto him, Yea, Lord; thou knowest that I love thee. He saith unto him, Feed my lambs. He saith to him again the second time, Simon, son of Jonas, lovest thou me? He saith unto him, Yea, Lord; thou knowest that I love thee. He saith unto him, Feed my sheep. He saith unto him the third time, Simon, son of Jonas, lovest thou me? Peter was grieved because he said unto him the third time, Lovest thou me? And he said unto him, Lord, thou knowest all things; thou knowest that I love thee. Jesus saith unto him, Feed my sheep.

Or this: St. Matt. xxviii, 18–20.

Jesus came and spake unto them, saying, All power is given unto me in heaven and in earth. Go ye therefore, and teach all nations, baptizing them in the name of the Father, and of the Son, and of the Holy Ghost: teaching them to observe all things whatsoever I have commanded you: and, lo, I am with you alway, even unto the end of the world.

After the Gospel and the sermon are ended, the elected person shall be presented by the two Elders unto the Bishop, saying,

We present unto you this holy man to be ordained a Bishop.

Then the Bishop shall move the congregation present to pray, saying thus to them:

Brethren, it is written in the Gospel of St. Luke, that our Saviour Christ continued the whole night in prayer before he did choose and send forth his twelve apostles. It is written also in the Acts of the Apostles, that the disciples who were at Antioch did fast and pray before they laid hands on Paul and Barnabas, and sent them forth. Let us, therefore, following the example of our Saviour Christ, and his apostles, first fall to prayer before we admit, and send forth this person presented to us, to the work whereunto we trust the Holy Ghost hath called him.

Then shall be said this prayer following.

Almighty God, Giver of all good things, who by thy Holy Spirit hast appointed divers orders of Ministers in thy Church: mercifully behold this thy servant now called to the work and ministry of a Bishop, and replenish him so with the truth of thy doctrine, and adorn him with innocency of life, that both by word and deed he may faithfully serve thee in this office, to the glory of thy name, and the edifying and well governing of thy Church, through the merits of our Saviour Jesus Christ, who liveth and reigneth with thee, and the Holy Ghost, world without end. *Amen.*

Then the Bishop shall say to him that is to be ordained,

Brother, forasmuch as the Holy Scripture commands that we should not be hasty in laying on hands, and admitting any person to government in the Church of Christ, which he hath purchased with no less price than the effusion of his own blood; before I admit you to this administration, I will examine you on certain articles, to the end that the congregation present may have a trial, and bear witness how you are minded to behave yourself in the Church of God.

Are you persuaded that you are truly called to this ministration, according to the will of our Lord Jesus Christ?

Answ. I am so persuaded.

The Bishop. Are you persuaded that the Holy Scriptures contain sufficiently all doctrine required of necessity for eternal salvation, through faith in Jesus Christ?

And are you determined, out of the same Holy Scriptures, to instruct the people committed to your charge, and to teach or maintain nothing as required of necessity to eternal salvation, but that which you shall be persuaded may be concluded and proved by the same?

Answ. I am so persuaded, and determined, by God's grace.

The Bishop. Will you then faithfully exercise yourself in the same Holy Scriptures, and call upon God by prayer for the true understanding of the same, so as you may be able by them to teach and exhort with wholesome doctrine, and to withstand and convince the gainsayers?

Answ. I will so do, by the help of God.

The Bishop. Are you ready with faithful diligence to banish and drive away all erroneous and strange doctrines contrary to God's word, and both privately and openly to call upon and encourage others to the same?

Answ. I am ready, the Lord being my helper.

The Bishop. Will you deny all ungodliness and worldly lust, and live soberly, righteously, and godly, in this present world, that you may show yourself in all things an example of good works unto others, that the adversary may be ashamed, having nothing to say against you?

Answ. I will so do, the Lord being my helper.

The Bishop. Will you maintain and set forward, as much as shall lie in you, quietness, love, and peace, among all men; and such as shall be unquiet, disobedient, and criminal, within your district, correct and punish according to such authority as you have by God's word, and as shall be committed unto you?

Answ. I will so do, by the help of God.

The Bishop. Will you be faithful in ordaining, sending, or laying hands upon others?

Answ. I will so be, by the help of God.

The Bishop. Will you show yourself gentle, and be merciful for Christ's sake, to poor and needy people, and to all strangers destitute of help?

Answ. I will so show myself, by God's help.

Then the Bishop shall say,

Almighty God, our heavenly Father, who hath given you a good will to do all these things, grant also unto you strength and power to perform the same; that he accomplishing in you the good work which he hath begun, you may be found perfect and irreprehensible at the last day, through Jesus Christ our Lord. *Amen.*

Then shall Veni, Creator Spiritus, be said.

Come, Holy Ghost, our souls inspire,
And lighten with celestial fire.
Thou the anointing Spirit art,
Who dost thy seven-fold gifts impart.
Thy blessed unction from above
Is comfort, life, and fire of love.
Enable with perpetual light
The dullness of our blinded sight;
Anoint and cheer our soilèd face
With the abundance of thy grace;
Keep far our foes, give peace at home;
Where thou art Guide, no ill can come.
Teach us to know the Father, Son,
And thee of both to be but one;
That through the ages all along,
This may be our endless song:
Praise to thy eternal merit,
Father, Son, and Holy Spirit.

That ended, the Bishop shall say,

Lord, hear our prayer.
Answ. And let our cry come unto thee.

Bishop. Let us pray.

Almighty God and most merciful Father, who of thine infinite goodness hast given thine only and dearly beloved Son Jesus Christ to be our Redeemer, and the Author of everlasting life; who after that he had made perfect our redemption by his death, and was ascended into heaven, poured down his gifts abundantly upon men, making some apostles, some prophets, some evangelists, some pastors and doctors, to the edifying and making perfect his Church: grant, we beseech thee, to this thy servant, such grace that he may evermore be ready to spread abroad thy Gospel, the glad tidings of reconciliation with thee, and use the authority given him, not to destruction, but to salvation; not to hurt, but to help; so that as a wise and faithful servant, giving to the family their portion in due season, he may at last be received into everlasting joy, through Jesus Christ our Lord, who, with thee and the Holy Ghost, liveth and reigneth, one God, world without end. *Amen.*

Then the Bishop and Elders present shall lay their hands upon the head of the elected person, kneeling before them upon his knees, the Bishop saying,

Receive the Holy Ghost for the office and work of a Bishop in the Church of God now committed unto thee by the imposition of our hands, in the name of the Father, and of the Son, and of the Holy Ghost. *Amen.* And remember that thou stir up the grace of God which is given thee by this imposition of our hands; for God hath not given us the spirit of fear, but of power, and love, and soberness.

Then the Bishop shall deliver him the Bible, saying,

Give heed unto reading, exhortation, and doctrine. Think upon the things contained in this book. Be diligent in them, that the increase coming thereby may be manifest unto all men. Take heed unto thyself, and to thy doctrine; for by so doing thou shalt both save thyself and them that hear thee. Be to the flock of Christ a shepherd, not a wolf: feed them, devour them not. Hold up the weak, heal the sick, bind up the broken, bring again the outcast, seek the lost; be so merciful that you may not be too remiss; so minister discipline that you forget not mercy; that when the chief Shepherd shall appear, you may receive the never-fading crown of glory, through Jesus Christ our Lord. *Amen.*

[Then the Bishop shall administer the Lord's Supper, with whom the newly ordained Bishop and other persons present shall communicate.]

Immediately before the benediction shall be said the following prayers:

Most merciful Father, we beseech thee to send down upon this thy servant thy heavenly blessing, and so endue him with thy Holy Spirit, that he, preaching thy word, may not only be earnest to reprove, beseech, and rebuke with all patience and doctrine, but also may be to such as believe a wholesome example in word, in conversation, in love, in faith, in chastity, and in purity; that faithfully fulfilling his course, at the latter day he may receive the crown of righteousness laid up by the Lord, the righteous Judge, who liveth and reigneth, one God with the Father and the Holy Ghost, world without end. *Amen.*

Prevent us, O Lord, in all our doings with thy most gracious favor, and further us with thy continual help, that in all our works begun, continued, and ended in thee, we may glorify thy holy name, and finally, by thy mercy, obtain everlasting life through Jesus Christ our Lord. *Amen.*

The peace of God, which passeth all understanding, keep your hearts and minds in the knowledge and love of God, and of his son Jesus Christ our Lord; and the blessing of God Almighty, the Father, the Son, and the Holy Ghost, be among you and remain with you always. *Amen.*

II. THE FORM AND MANNER OF ORDAINING ELDERS.

[When the day appointed by the Bishop is come, there shall be a sermon or exhortation, declaring the duty and office of such as come to be admitted Elders; how necessary that order is in the Church of Christ, and also how the people ought to esteem them in their office.]

After which, one of the Elders shall present unto the Bishop all them that are to be ordained, and say,

I PRESENT unto you these persons present to be ordained Elders.

Then their names being read aloud, the Bishop shall say unto the people,

Brethren, these are they whom we purpose, God willing, this day to ordain elders. For after due examination we find not to the contrary, but that they are lawfully called to this function and ministry, and that they are persons meet for the same. But if there be any of you who knoweth any impediment or crime in any of them, for the which he ought not to be received into this holy ministry, let him come forth in the name of God, and show what the crime or impediment is.

[If any crime or impediment be objected, the Bishop shall surcease from ordaining that person until such time as the party accused shall be found clear of the crime.]

Then shall be said the Collect, Epistle, and Gospel, as followeth.

The Collect.

Almighty God, Giver of all good things, who by thy Holy Spirit hast appointed divers orders of Ministers in thy Church: mercifully behold these thy servants now called to the office of Elders, and replenish them so with the truth of thy doctrine, and adorn them with innocency of life, that both by word and good example they may faithfully serve thee in this office, to the glory of thy name, and the edification of thy Church, through the merits of our Saviour Jesus Christ, who liveth and reigneth with thee and the Holy Ghost, world without end. *Amen.*

The Epistle. Eph. iv, 7–13.

Unto every one of us is given grace according to the measure of the gift of Christ. Wherefore he saith, When he ascended up on high, he led captivity captive, and gave gifts unto men. Now that he ascended, what is it but that he also descended first into the lower parts of the earth? He that descended is the same also that ascended up far above all heavens, that he might fill all things. And he gave some, apostles; and some, prophets; and some, evangelists; and some, pastors and teachers; for the perfecting of the saints, for the work of the ministry, for the edifying of the body of Christ, till we all come in the unity of the faith, and of the knowledge of the Son of God, unto a perfect man, unto the measure of the stature of the fullness of Christ.

After this shall be read for the Gospel, part of the tenth chapter of St. John.

St. John x, 1–16.

Verily, verily, I say unto you, He that entereth not by the door into the sheepfold, but climbeth up some other way, the same is a thief and a robber. But he that entereth in by the door is the shepherd of the sheep. To him the porter openeth; and the sheep hear his voice: and he calleth his own sheep by name, and leadeth them out. And when he putteth forth his own sheep, he goeth before them, and the sheep follow him, for they know his voice. And a *stranger will they not follow*, but will flee from him, for they know not the voice of strangers. This parable spake Jesus unto them; but they understood not what things they were which he spake unto them. Then said Jesus unto them again, Verily, verily, I say unto you, I am the door of the sheep. All that ever came before me are thieves and robbers: but the sheep did not hear them. I am the door: by me if any man enter in, he shall be saved, and shall go in and out, and find pasture. The thief cometh not but for to steal, and to kill, and to destroy; I am come that they might have life, and that they might have it more abundantly. I am the good Shepherd: the good Shepherd giveth his life for the sheep. But he that is a hireling, and not the shepherd, whose own the sheep are not, seeth the wolf coming, and leaveth the sheep, and fleeth; and the wolf catcheth them, and scattereth the sheep. The hireling fleeth, because he is a hireling, and careth not for the sheep. I am the good Shepherd, and know my sheep, and am known of mine. As the Father knoweth me, even so know I the Father: and I lay down my life for the sheep. And other sheep I have, which are not of this fold:

them also I must bring, and they shall hear my voice, and there shall be one fold and one shepherd.

And that done, the Bishop shall say unto them as hereafter followeth:

You have heard, brethren, as well in your private examination as in the exhortation which was now made to you, and in the holy lessons taken out of the Gospel, and the writings of the apostles, of what dignity and of how great importance this office is whereunto ye are called. And now again we exhort you, in the name of our Lord Jesus Christ, that you have in remembrance unto how high a dignity and to how weighty an office ye are called: that is to say, to be messengers, watchmen, and stewards of the Lord, to teach and to premonish, to feed and provide for the Lord's family, to seek for Christ's sheep that are dispersed abroad, and for his children who are in the midst of this evil world, that they may be saved through Christ forever.

Have always, therefore, printed in your remembrance how great a treasure is committed to your charge. For they are the sheep of Christ, which he bought with his death, and for whom he shed his blood. The Church and congregation whom you must serve, is his spouse and his body. And if it shall happen, the same Church, or any member thereof, do take any hurt or hinderance by reason of your negligence, ye know the greatness of the fault, and also the horrible punishment that will ensue. Wherefore consider with yourselves the end of the ministry toward the children of God, toward the spouse and body of Christ; and see that you never cease your labor, your care and diligence, until you have done all that lieth in you, according to your bounden duty, to bring all such as are or shall be committed to your charge, unto that agreement in the faith and knowledge of God, and to that ripeness and perfectness of age in Christ, that there be no place left among you, either for error in religion, or for viciousness in life.

Forasmuch, then, as your office is both of so great excellency, and of so great difficulty, ye see with how great care and study ye ought to apply yourselves, as well that ye may show yourselves dutiful and thankful unto that Lord who hath placed you in so high a dignity; as also to beware that neither you yourselves offend, nor be occasion that others offend. Howbeit ye cannot have a mind and will thereto of yourselves, for that will and ability is given of God alone: therefore ye ought, and have need to pray earnestly for his Holy Spirit. And seeing that ye cannot by any other means compass the doing of so weighty a work, pertaining to the salvation of man, but with doctrine and exhortation taken out of the Holy Scriptures, and with a life agreeable to the same; consider how studious ye ought to be in reading and learning the Scriptures, and in framing the manners both of yourselves and of them that specially pertain unto you, according to the rule of the same Scriptures; and for this self-same cause, how ye ought to forsake and set aside (as much as you may) all worldly cares and studies.

We have good hope that you have all weighed and pondered these things with yourselves long before this time: and that you have clearly determined, by God's grace, to give yourselves wholly to this office, whereunto it hath pleased God to call you: so that, as much as lieth in you, you will apply yourselves wholly to this one thing, and draw all your cares and studies this way; and that you will continually pray to God the Father, by the mediation of our only Saviour Jesus Christ, for the heavenly assistance of the Holy Ghost; that by daily reading and weighing of the Scriptures, ye may wax riper and stronger in your ministry; and that ye may so endeavor yourselves from time to time to sanctify the lives of you and yours, and to fashion them after the rule and doctrine of Christ, that ye may be wholesome and godly examples and patterns for the people to follow.

And now that this present congregation of Christ here assembled, may also understand your minds and wills in these things, and that this your promise may the more move you to do your duties, ye shall answer plainly to these things which we, in the name of God and his Church, shall demand of you touching the same.

Do you think in your heart that you are truly called, according to the will of our Lord Jesus Christ, to the order of Elders?

Answ. I think so.

The Bishop. Are you persuaded that the Holy Scriptures contain sufficiently all doctrine required of necessity for eternal salvation through faith in Jesus Christ? And are you determined out of the said Scriptures to instruct the people committed to your charge, and to teach nothing as required of necessity to eternal salvation, but that which you shall be persuaded may be concluded and proved by the Scripture?

Answ. I am so persuaded, and have so determined, by God's grace.

The Bishop. Will you then give your faithful diligence always so to minister the doctrine, and sacraments, and discipline of Christ, as the Lord hath commanded?

Ans. I will so do, by the help of the Lord.

The Bishop. Will you be ready with all faithful diligence to banish and drive away all erroneous and strange doctrines contrary to God's word; and to use both public and private monitions and exhortations, as well to the sick as to the whole within your charge, as need shall require and occasion shall be given?

Answ. I will, the Lord being my helper.

The Bishop. Will you be diligent in prayers, and in reading of the Holy Scriptures, and in such studies as help to the knowledge of the same, laying aside the study of the world and the flesh?

Answ. I will endeavor so to do, the Lord being my helper.

The Bishop. Will you be diligent to frame and fashion yourselves, and your families, according to the doctrine of Christ; and to make both yourselves and them, as much as in you lieth, wholesome examples and patterns to the flock of Christ?

Answ. I shall apply myself thereto, the Lord being my helper.

The Bishop. Will you maintain and set forward, as much as lieth in you, quietness, peace, and love, among all Christian people, and especially among them that are or shall be committed to your charge?

Answ. I will so do, the Lord being my helper.

The Bishop. Will you reverently obey your chief Ministers, unto whom is committed the charge and government over you; following with a glad mind and will their godly admonitions, submitting yourselves to their godly judgments?

Answ. I will so do, the Lord being my helper.

Then shall the Bishop, standing up, say,

Almighty God, who hath given you this will to do all these things, grant also unto you strength and power to perform the same; that he may accomplish his work which he hath begun in you, through Jesus Christ our Lord. *Amen.*

[After this the congregation shall be desired secretly in their prayers to make their humble supplications to God for all these things; for the which prayers there shall be silence kept for a space.]

After which shall be said by the Bishop, (the persons to be ordained Elders all kneeling,) Veni, Creator, Spiritus, *the Bishop beginning and the Elders and others that are present answering by verse as followeth:*

Come, Holy Ghost, our souls inspire,
And lighten with celestial fire.
Thou the anointing Spirit art,
Who dost thy sevenfold gifts impart.
Thy blessed unction from above
Is comfort, life, and fire of love.
Enable with perpetual light
The dullness of our blinded sight;
Anoint and cheer our soilèd face
With the abundance of thy grace;
Keep far our foes, give peace at home;
Where thou art Guide, no ill can come.
Teach us to know the Father, Son,
And thee of both to be but one;

That through the ages all along,
This may be our endless song:
Praise to thy eternal merit,
Father, Son, and Holy Spirit.

That done, the Bishop shall pray in this wise, and say,

Let us pray.

Almighty God and Heavenly Father, who of thine infinite love and goodness toward us, hast given to us thy only and most dearly beloved Son Jesus Christ to be our Redeemer, and the Author of everlasting life; who, after he had made perfect our redemption by his death, and was ascended into heaven, sent abroad into the world his apostles, prophets, evangelists, doctors, and pastors, by whose labor and ministry he gathered together a great flock in all parts of the world, to set forth the eternal praise of thy holy name: for these so great benefits of thy eternal goodness, and for that thou hast vouchsafed to call these thy servants here present to the same office and ministry appointed for the salvation of mankind, we render unto thee most hearty thanks; we praise and worship thee; and we humbly beseech thee by the same, thy blessed Son, to grant unto all who either here or elsewhere call upon thy name, that we may continue to show ourselves thankful unto thee for these and all other thy benefits; and that we may daily increase and go forward in the knowledge and faith of thee and thy Son, by the Holy Spirit: so that as well by these thy ministers, as by them over whom they shall be appointed thy ministers, thy holy name may be forever glorified, and thy blessed kingdom enlarged, through the same, thy Son Jesus Christ our Lord, who liveth and reigneth with thee in the unity of the same Holy Spirit, world without end. *Amen.*

When this prayer is done, the Bishop, with the Elders present, shall lay their hands severally upon the head of every one that receiveth the order of Elders; the receivers humbly kneeling upon their knees, and the Bishop saying,

The Lord pour upon thee the Holy Ghost for the office and work of an Elder in the Church of God, now committed unto thee by the imposition of our hands. And be thou a faithful dispenser of the word of God, and of his holy sacraments; in the name of the Father, and of the Son, and of the Holy Ghost. *Amen.*

Then the Bishop shall deliver to every one of them kneeling, the Bible into his hands, saying,

Take thou authority to preach the word of God, and to administer the holy sacraments in the congregation.

Then the Bishop shall say,

Most merciful Father, we beseech thee to send upon these thy servants thy heavenly blessings, that they may be clothed with righteousness; and that thy word spoken by their mouths may have such success, that it may never be spoken in vain. Grant also that we may have grace to hear and receive what they shall deliver out of thy most holy word, or agreeably to the same, as the means of our salvation; and that in all our words and deeds we may seek thy glory, and the increase of thy kingdom, through Jesus Christ our Lord. *Amen.*

Prevent us, O Lord, in all our doings, with thy most gracious favor, and further us with thy continual help, that in all our works begun, continued, and ended in thee, we may glorify thy holy name, and finally, by thy mercy, obtain everlasting life, through Jesus Christ our Lord. *Amen.*

The peace of God, which passeth all understanding, keep your hearts and minds in the knowledge and love of God, and of his Son Jesus Christ our Lord; and the blessing of God Almighty, the Father, the Son, and the Holy Ghost, be among you, and remain with you always. *Amen.*

*** [If on the same day the order of Deacons be given to some, and that of Elders to others, the Deacons shall be first presented, and then the Elders. The collects shall both be used; first that for Deacons, then that for Elders. The epistle shall be Ephesians iv, 7–13, as before in this office. Immediately after which, they that are to be ordained Deacons shall be examined and ordained as is above prescribed. Then one of them having read the Gospel—which shall be St. John x, 1, as before in this office—they that are to be ordained Elders shall likewise be examined and ordained, as in this office before appointed.]

III.—THE FORM AND MANNER OF MAKING DEACONS.

[When the day appointed by the Bishop is come, there shall be a sermon or exhortation, declaring the duty and office of such as come to be admitted Deacons.]

After which, one of the Elders shall present unto the Bishop the persons to be ordained Deacons, and their names being read aloud, the Bishop shall say unto the people:

BRETHREN, if there be any of you who knoweth any impediment or crime in any of these persons presented to be ordained Deacons, for the which he ought not to be admitted to that office, let him come forth in the name of God, and show what the crime or impediment is.

[If any crime or impediment be objected, the Bishop shall surcease from ordaining that person, until such time as the party accused shall be found clear of that crime.]

Then shall be read the following collect and epistle.

The Collect.

Almighty God, who by thy Divine providence hast appointed divers orders of ministers in thy Church, and didst inspire thy apostles to choose into the order of Deacons thy first martyr, St. Stephen, with others; mercifully behold these thy servants, now called to the like office and administration; replenish them so with the truth of thy doctrine, and adorn them with innocency of life, that both by word and good example they may faithfully serve thee in this office to the glory of thy name, and the edification of thy Church, through the merits of our Saviour Jesus Christ, who liveth and reigneth with thee and the Holy Ghost now and forever. *Amen.*

The Epistle. 1 Tim. iii, 8–13.

Likewise must the Deacons be grave, not double-tongued, not given to much wine, not greedy of filthy lucre; holding the mystery of the faith in a pure conscience. And let these also first be proved; then let them use the office of a Deacon, being found blameless. Even so must their wives be grave, not slanderers, sober, faithful in all things. Let the Deacons be the husbands of one wife, ruling their children and their own houses well. For they that have used the office of a Deacon well, purchase to themselves a good degree, and great boldness in the faith which is in Christ Jesus.

Then shall the Bishop examine every one of those who are to be ordained, in the presence of the people, after this manner following:

Do you trust that you are inwardly moved by the Holy Ghost to take upon you the office of the ministry in the Church of Christ, to serve God for the promoting of his glory and the edifying of his people?

Answ. I trust so.

The Bishop. Do you unfeignedly believe all the canonical Scriptures of the Old and New Testament?

Answ. I do believe them.

The Bishop. Will you diligently read or expound the same unto the people whom you shall be appointed to serve?

Answ. I will.

The Bishop. It appertaineth to the office

of a Deacon to assist the Elder in divine service; and especially when he ministereth the holy communion, to help him in the distribution thereof, and to read and expound the Holy Scriptures; to instruct the youth, and, in the absence of the Elder, to baptize. And furthermore, it is his office to search for the sick, poor, and impotent, that they may be visited and relieved. Will you do this gladly and willingly?

Answ. I will do so by the help of God.

The Bishop. Will you apply all your diligence to frame and fashion your own lives (and the lives of your families) according to the doctrine of Christ; and to make (both) yourselves, (and them,) as much as in you lieth, wholesome examples of the flock of Christ?

Answ. I will do so, the Lord being my helper.

The Bishop. Will you reverently obey them to whom the charge and government over you is committed, following with a glad mind and will their godly admonitions?

Answ. I will endeavor so to do, the Lord being my helper.

Then the Bishop, laying his hands severally upon the head of every one of them, shall say,

Take thou authority to execute the office of a Deacon in the Church of God; in the name of the Father, and of the Son, and of the Holy Ghost. *Amen.*

Then shall the Bishop deliver to every one of them the Holy Bible, saying,

Take thou authority to read the Holy Scriptures in the Church of God, and to preach the same.

Then one of them appointed by the Bishop shall read the Gospel.

Luke xii, 35–38.

Let your loins be girded about, and your lights burning, and ye yourselves like unto men that wait for their Lord, when he will return from the wedding, that when he cometh and knocketh, they may open unto him immediately. Blessed are those servants whom the Lord when he cometh shall find watching. Verily I say unto you, that he shall gird himself, and make them to sit down to meat, and will come forth and serve them. And if he shall come in the second watch, or come in the third watch, and find them so, blessed are those servants.

[Then shall the Bishop proceed in the communion, and all that are ordained shall receive the holy communion.]

The communion ended, immediately before the benediction shall be said these collects following.

Almighty God, Giver of all good things, who of thy great goodness hast vouchsafed to accept and take these thy servants into the office of Deacons in thy Church; make them, we beseech thee, O Lord, to be modest, humble, and constant in their ministration, and to have a ready will to observe all spiritual discipline; that they, having always the testimony of a good conscience, and continuing ever stable and strong in thy Son Christ, may so well behave themselves in this inferior office, that they may be found worthy to be called into the higher ministries in thy Church, through the same, thy Son our Saviour Jesus Christ; to whom be glory and honor, world without end. *Amen.*

Prevent us, O Lord, in all our doings, with thy most gracious favor, and further us with thy continual help; that in all our works begun, continued, and ended in thee, we may glorify thy holy name, and finally, by thy mercy, obtain everlasting life, through Jesus Christ our Lord. *Amen.*

The peace of God, which passeth all understanding, keep your hearts and minds in the knowledge and love of God, and of his Son Jesus Christ our Lord; and the blessing of God Almighty, the Father, the Son, and the Holy Ghost be among you, and remain with you always. *Amen.*

PART IV.

BENEVOLENT INSTITUTIONS.

SECTION I.

Sunday-schools and the Instruction of Children.

Quest. 1. WHAT shall we do for the moral and religious instruction of the children?

Answ. 1. It shall be the special duty of Preachers having charge of circuits or stations, with the aid of the other Preachers, to form Sunday-schools in all our congregations where ten children can be collected for that purpose; and to engage the cooperation of as many of our members as they can, to visit the schools as often as practicable; to preach on the subject of Sunday-schools and religious instruction in each congregation at least once in six months; and to form Bible classes wherever they can for the instruction of larger children, youth, and adults; and where they cannot superintend them personally, to see that suitable teachers are provided for that purpose.

2. It shall also be the duty of Preachers to enforce faithfully upon parents and Sunday-school teachers the great importance of instructing children in the doctrines and duties of our holy religion, to see that our Catechisms be used as extensively as possible both in our Sunday-schools and families, to preach to the children, and publicly catechise them in the Sunday-schools and at special meetings appointed for that purpose.

3. It shall be the duty of every preacher in his pastoral visits to pay special attention to the children, speaking to them personally and kindly on the subject of experimental and practical godliness, according to their capacity, pray earnestly for them, and diligently instruct and exhort all parents to dedicate their children to the Lord in baptism as early as convenient.

4. Each Preacher in charge shall lay before the Quarterly Conference,* to be entered on its Journal, the number and state of the Sunday-schools and Bible classes in his charge, and the extent to which he has preached to the children and

* See part ii, chapter ii, section 12,—ED.

catechised them, and make the required report on Sunday-schools to his Annual Conference.

5. It is recommended that each Annual Conference, where the general state of the work will allow, request the appointment of a special agent, to travel throughout its bounds, for the purpose of promoting the interests of Sunday-schools; and his expenses shall be paid out of collections which he shall be directed to make, or otherwise, as shall be ordered by the conference.

SECTION II.

The Support of Missions.

1. The support of missions is committed to the Churches, congregations, and societies as such.

2. It shall be the duty of each Annual Conference, where missions have been or are to be established, to appoint a standing committee, (which shall keep a record of its doings, and report the same to its conference,) whose duty it shall be, in conjunction with the President of the Conference, to make an estimate of the amount necessary for the support of each mission and mission school, in addition to the regular allowance

of the Discipline to Preachers and their families from year to year: for which amount the President of the Conference for the time being shall draw on the treasurer of the society in quarterly installments.

3. It shall be the duty of each Annual Conference to form within its bounds a Conference Missionary Society, which shall appoint its own officers, fix the terms of membership, and otherwise regulate its own administration. But it shall pay all its funds into the treasury of the Parent Society.

4. It shall be the duty of each Presiding Elder to bring the subject of our missions before the Quarterly Conference of each circuit and station within his district at the last Quarterly Conference in each year; and said conference shall proceed to appoint a committee, of not less than *three* nor more than *nine*, (of which the Preacher in charge shall be chairman,) to be called the Committee on Missions, whose duty it shall be to aid the Preacher in charge in carrying into effect the disciplinary measures for the support of our missions.

5. It shall be the duty of the Preacher in charge, aided by the Committee on Missions, to provide for the diffusion of mis-

sionary intelligence in the Church and congregation.

6. It shall be the duty of the Preacher in charge, aided by the Committee on Missions, to institute a monthly missionary prayer-meeting, or lecture, in each society, or Church and congregation, wherever practicable, for the purpose of imploring the Divine blessing on missions; for the diffusion of missionary intelligence, and to afford an opportunity for voluntary offerings to the missionary cause.

7. It shall be the duty of the preacher in charge, aided by the Committee on Missions, to appoint missionary collectors, and furnish them with suitable books and instructions, that they may call on each member of the society, or Church and congregation, and on other persons, at their discretion, for his or her annual, semi-annual, quarterly, monthly, or weekly contributions for the support of missions. Said collectors shall make monthly returns (unless otherwise instructed by the committee) to the Preacher in charge, or to the Missionary Treasurer of the Church, if there be such treasurer appointed by the Committee on Missions. Such returns shall be fairly entered in a book, which the com-

mittee shall provide, together with collections and contributions received from other sources. Such entries shall set forth the name of each collector, the real or assumed names of the contributors to each collector, with the amount contributed by each.

8. Each Preacher in charge shall report at Conference, to the Executive Committee, or Board of Managers of the Conference Missionary Society, a plain transcript of the record of the returns provided for in section seven, comprehending the name of each collector in his charge, and the name, real or assumed, of each contributor to each collector of *fifty cents* or upward during the year; and the aggregate sum of all contributions under fifty cents each, that they may be by said Executive Committee, or Board of Managers, properly arranged by districts, and by charges, for publication in the Annual Report of the Conference Missionary Society; together with the contributions and collections received from other sources, unless the Conference shall by vote declare such transcript returns, and such publication, not to be advisable.

9. It shall be the duty of the Preacher in charge, with the aid of the Committee

on Missions, to present once in the year to the Societies, or the Churches and congregations, the cause of missions, and to ask public collections and contributions for the support of the same. The manner of asking and taking such collections and contributions shall be at the discretion of the pastor and the Committee on Missions, with this injunction, that the pastor shall preach, or cause to be preached on the occasion, one or more sermons; and with the recommendation that one whole Sabbath day be given to the cause, on this annual presentation of missions, in our principal Churches and congregations.

10. It is earnestly recommended that each Sunday-school in our Churches and congregations be organized into a Missionary Society, under such rules and regulations as the pastor, the superintendent, and teachers may prescribe.

11. Each Annual Conference shall designate the month or months in which the public collections and contributions for missions shall be taken within its bounds.

12. The President of the Conference, at each session, shall appoint one of its members, with an alternate, to preach a missionary sermon during its next succeeding ses-

sion, at such time and place as the officers of the Conference Missionary Society shall designate, and said officers shall cause timely notice of such sermon to be published abroad.

13. It shall be the duty of each Presiding Elder to see that the foregoing provisions are faithfully executed in his district; and in order thereto, he shall inquire at each session of the Quarterly Conference what has been done by the Mission Committee toward raising funds for the support of missions during the preceding quarter, and particularly whether the Sunday-schools have been organized into Missionary Societies.

14. When the character of the Presiding Elder is under examination, the Bishop shall ask him whether the provisions of the Discipline for the support of missions have been carried out on his district: and when the character of a preacher in charge is examined, inquire of him what amount has been raised on his charge for missions.

15. The Corresponding Secretary of the Missionary Society of the Methodist Episcopal Church shall be a member of such Annual Conference as he may, with the approbation of the Bishops, select.

16. Any Annual Conference may, at its option, by a vote of two thirds of its members, assume the responsibility of supporting such missions, already established within its own limits, as have hitherto been reported under the head of "Missions in the Destitute Portions of the Regular Work;" and for this purpose it shall be at liberty to organize a Conference Domestic Society, with branches; *provided* such organization shall not interfere with the collections for the Missionary Society of the Methodist Episcopal Church, as required by the Discipline. *Provided, also,* that in case more funds shall be raised for such missions than are needed, the surplus shall be paid over to the Treasurer of the Parent Society of the Methodist Episcopal Church, at New York, to be appropriated to such mission or missions, under the care of the Society, as may be designated by said Conference.

SECTION III.

Printing and Circulation of Religious Tracts.

Provision is made for the publication at the Book Concern of cheap books and tracts, in our own and foreign languages. For the duties of the Editor of Tracts and Corresponding Secretary of the Tract Society, see part iv, sect. v. Our Tract Society is designed to aid in the diffusion of religious knowledge by the circulation of our evangelical publications.

1. It is recommended to our people everywhere to form Tract Societies, auxiliary to the Tract Society of the Methodist Episcopal Church.

2. It is recommended to preachers in charge to make annually, in their several congregations, collections in behalf of the Tract Society of the Methodist Episcopal Church.

SECTION IV.

The Chartered Fund.

Quest. 1. What further provision shall be made for the distressed Traveling Preachers, for the families of Traveling Preachers, and for the Superannuated and Worn-out Preachers, and the widows and orphans of Preachers?

Answ. There shall be a Chartered Fund, to be supported by the voluntary contributions of our friends: the principal stock of which shall be funded under the direction of trustees chosen by the General Conference, and the interest applied under the direction of the General Conference, according to the following regulations, namely:

1. The Elders, and those who have the oversight of circuits, shall be collectors and receivers of subscriptions, etc., for this fund.

2. The money shall, if possible, be conveyed by bills of exchange, or otherwise, through the means of the post, to the general Book Agents, who shall pay it to the trustees of the fund: otherwise it shall be brought to the ensuing Annual Conference.

3. The interest shall be divided into forty-nine parts, and each of the Annual Conferences shall have authority to draw one forty-ninth part out of the fund; and if in one or more Conferences a part less than one forty-ninth be drawn out of the fund in any given year, then in such case or cases, the other Annual Conferences, held in the same year, shall have authority, if they judge it necessary, to draw out of the fund such surplus of the interest which has not been applied by the former Conferences; and the Bishops shall bring the necessary information of the state of the interest of the fund, respecting the year in question, from Conference to Conference.

4. All drafts on the Chartered Fund shall be made on the President of the said fund, by order of the Annual Conference, signed

by the President, and countersigned by the Secretary of the said Conference.

5. The money subscribed for the Chartered Fund may be lodged, on proper securities, in the States respectively in which it has been subscribed, under the direction of deputies living in such States respectively; *provided* such securities and such deputies be proposed as shall be approved of by the trustees in Philadelphia; and the stock in which it is proposed to lodge the money be sufficiently productive to give satisfaction to the trustees.

Quest. 2. How shall vacancies in the Board of Trustees of the Chartered Fund be filled?

Answ. The Board of Trustees shall have power to fill any vacancy or vacancies that may occur in their body by death, resignation, or otherwise, subject, however, to the approval of the first General Conference that may be held after such vacancy or vacancies shall have occurred.

SECTION V.

Printing and Circulating Books, Tracts, and Periodicals.

1. The principal establishments of the Book Concern shall be in the cities of New York and Cincinnati; the Agents of our principal establishments at New York and Cincinnati, and the Editors of our books and periodicals to be elected by the General Conference; and there shall be such other establishments as the General Conference may deem expedient.

2. There shall be an Agent and an Assistant Agent, both of whom shall be chosen from among the Traveling Preachers, and shall be members of such Conferences as they may, with the approbation of the Bishops, select.

3. The Agents shall have authority to regulate the publications and all other parts of the business of the Concern, except what belongs to the editorial departments, as the state of the finances will admit, and the demands may require. It shall be their duty to send an exhibit of the state of the Book Concern at New York to each session of the Annual Con-

ferences, and report quadrennially to the General Conference.

4. They shall publish such books and tracts as are recommended by the General Conference, and may, if approved by the Editors, publish such as are recommended by the Book Committee at New York, or recommended by an Annual Conference; and they may reprint any book or tract which has been once approved and published by us, when in their judgment, and in the judgment of the Editors, the same ought to be reprinted; or they may publish any new work which may be approved by the Editors.

5. There shall be an Editor of the Methodist Quarterly Review and general books, and an Editor for the Christian Advocate and Journal, who, if chosen from among the Traveling Preachers, shall be members of such Conferences as they may, with the approbation of the Bishops, select. There shall be an Editor at New York of Sunday-school and Tract Publications, whose duty it shall be, in consultation with the Book Agents, to superintend all such publications issued at our Book Room, and to have charge of the Sunday-School Advocate or other Sunday-school and Tract

periodicals; and he shall be subject to the same regulations and restrictions which govern the other editors in New York. The Editor of Sunday-school publications shall also be the Corresponding Secretary of our Sunday-School Union, and of the Tract Society.

6. The Book Committee at New York shall consist of seven Traveling Ministers,* to be chosen by the General Conference. During the intervals of the General Conference, they shall have power to fill any vacancy that may occur in their own body. It shall be the duty of the Book Committee to examine into the condition of the Book Concern, to inspect the accounts of the Agents, and make a report thereof yearly to all the Annual Conferences, and to the General Conference. They shall also attend to such matters as may be referred to them by the Editors or Agent for their action or counsel. And they shall have power to suspend an Editor or Agent from his official relation as such, if they judge it necessary for the interests of the Church and the Concern. And a time shall be fixed, at as early a day as practicable, for the investigation of the official conduct of the said Editor or

[* See Appendix C.—ED.]

Agent, at which two or more of the Bishops shall be requested to attend; and by the concurrence of the Bishops present, and of a majority of the Committee, he may be removed from office in the interval of the General Conference. And in case a vacancy occurs in any of the agencies or editorial departments authorized by the General Conference, it shall be the duty of the Book Committee, and two or more of the General Superintendents, as soon as practicable, to provide for such vacancy until the next General Conference.

7. There shall be an Agent and an Assistant Agent to conduct the Western Book Concern in Cincinnati, to be chosen from among the Traveling Preachers, who shall manage the business in the western country, so as to co-operate with the Agents at New York, and shall be members of such Conferences as they may, with the approbation of the Bishops, select.

(1.) They shall have authority to publish any book or tract which has been previously published by the Agents at New York, when, in their judgment, and in the judgment of the Book Committee, the demand for such publication will justify, and the interests of the Church require it. *Provided*, they shall not reprint our large works, such as the Commentaries, quarto Bible, Wesley's and Fletcher's Works, or any other work, containing more than seven hundred pages. And the Agents at New York shall fill the orders for the Agents at Cincinnati for the plates of such books or tracts; and when the Agents at New York are about to issue any new work of less than seven hundred pages, they shall, when practicable, give notice to the Agents at Cincinnati, and furnish, if ordered by them, duplicate plates, which, with the above, shall be at cost.

(2.) They shall publish such books and tracts as are recommended to them for publication by the General Conference; and they may publish any new work which shall be approved by the Editors; and may publish any work recommended by the Book Committee at Cincinnati, or by an Annual Conference, if approved by the Editors.

(3.) Printed sheets ordered by the Agents from New York shall be sent at fifty per cent., and bound books of the General Catalogue at forty per cent., discount from the retail prices; and those ordered from

Cincinnati to New York to be sent on the same terms, the agency sending the books to be charged with the expense of transportation.

(4.) It shall be the duty of the Agents to send an exhibit of the state of the Book Concern at Cincinnati to each session of all the Annual Conferences, and report quadrennially to the General Conference.

(5.) The Book Committee of this department of the Book Concern shall consist of eleven Traveling Ministers,* to be chosen by the General Conference, whose powers and duties in reference to this establishment, embracing the Northwestern Christian Advocate, published at Chicago, Illinois, and the Central Christian Advocate, published at St. Louis, Missouri, shall be the same as those of the Book Committee at New York in relation to the Concern there.

(6.) The Agents of this establishment shall remit to the Agents at New York during the current year as largely and frequently as their funds will allow, and to the full amount of stock furnished, if practicable. They shall also pay one third of the salaries and traveling expenses of the

[* See Appendix D.—ED.]

Bishops, and also the same proportion of all other appropriations made by the said General Conference, unless otherwise ordered by said Conference.

(7.) There shall be an Editor of the Ladies' Repository, general books and tracts, except those in the German language, and an Editor of the Western, Northwestern, and Central Christian Advocates, who, if chosen from among the Traveling Preachers, shall be members of such Conferences as they may, with the approbation of the Bishops, select.

(8.) There shall be an Editor in the German department, who shall have charge of the Christian Apologist, and Sunday-School Bell, and perform all the editorial duties necessary in the printing of such books and tracts as may be recommended to the Agents as above, for publication in the German language.

8. Every Annual Conference shall appoint a committee, who, in the absence of the Agent, shall attend to the collection of the accounts sent out from the Book Concern, and return an accurate report of the same.

Every Presiding Elder, Minister, and Preacher, shall do everything in his power to recover all debts due to the Concern, for books or periodicals, within the bounds of his charge. If any person, Preacher or member, be indebted to the Book Concern, and refuse or neglect to make payment, or to come to a just settlement, let him be dealt with in the same manner as is directed in other cases of debt and disputed accounts.

9. Whenever a member of an Annual Conference applies for a location, it shall be asked in all cases, Is he indebted to the Book Concern? and if it be ascertained that he is, the Conference shall require him to secure said debt, if they judge it at all necessary or proper, before they grant him a location. Whenever any claimant on the funds of a Conference shall be in debt to the Book Concern, the Conference of which he is a member shall have power to appropriate the amount of such claim, or any part thereof, to the payment of said debt.

10. There shall also be published the Pittsburgh Christian Advocate at Pittsburgh, Pa.; the Northern Christian Advocate in Western New York; the Pacific Christian Advocate in Portland, Oregon; and the California Christian Advocate at San Fran-

cisco, California. There shall also be for each of these papers a separate Publishing Committee, whose duties shall be similar with regard to them to those of the Book Agents and Book Committees at New York and Cincinnati in relation to the publications under their care, so far as they may be applicable to the establishments under their supervision.

11. The Publishing Committee of the Pittsburgh Christian Advocate shall consist of three members from Pittsburgh Conference, two from the Erie Conference, and two from Western Virginia Conference, to be chosen by the General Conference.

12. The publishing Committee of the Northern Christian Advocate shall consist of one member from each of the following Conferences, to be chosen annually by the Conferences respectively, namely: Genesee, East Genesee, Oneida, Black River, and Wyoming Conferences.

13. The Publishing Committee of the Pacific Christian Advocate shall consist of five members of the Oregon Conference, to be chosen annually by said Conference.

The Publishing Committee of the California Christian Advocate shall consist of five members of the California Conference, to be chosen annually by said Conference.

14. The Publishing Committee in each of these establishments shall keep an account of the receipts and expenditures for the paper, correspond with the Agents at New York, hold all moneys, after defraying current expenses, subject to their order, and shall report annually on the state of the establishment to their Conference, and to the Agents at New York. And whenever it shall be found that such papers do not fully support themselves, with such aid as may have been allowed them, it shall be the duty of the Publishing Committees to discontinue them.

15. The Annual Conferences are affectionately and earnestly requested not to establish any more Conference papers; and where such papers exist, they may be discontinued when it can be done consistently with existing obligations.

16. There shall be a depository of our books at Pittsburgh, Pa.; at Boston, Mass.; and at Buffalo, N. Y., furnished by the Agents at New York with full supplies of the books of our General Catalogue, Sunday-school books, and Tracts, to be sold for the Concern on the same terms as at

New York. *Provided*, that there shall not be more than fifteen thousand dollars' worth at Pittsburgh, nor more than ten thousand dollars' worth at Boston. There shall also be a depository at Chicago, Ill., and one at St. Louis, Mo., to be supplied by the Agents at Cincinnati.

17. The expenses incident to the transportation, management, and sale of our books at these depositories having been met out of the sales, according to an arrangement with the Agents, the net proceeds shall be forwarded to said Agents as fast as possible.

18. Full statements shall be made to the Agents semi-annually, at dates fixed by them, of the amount of sales and of expenses; distinguishing cash sales from those on credit. And, also, annual statements shall be made of the amount of stock.

19. If it shall appear to the Agents that the business at either of the depositories is not well managed, or that remittances are not duly made, they shall immediately correct the error complained of; or, with the concurrence of the Book Committee, cause the affairs of the Depository to be wound up.

to obtain their allowance from the people where they have labored may present a claim to the Conference, to be paid out of the money at the disposal of the Conference, and such claim may be paid, or any part thereof, as the Conference may determine.

SECTION II.

Building and Renting Houses for the Use of Traveling Preachers.

Quest. What advice or direction shall be given concerning the building or renting of dwelling-houses for the use of the married Traveling Preachers?

Answ. 1. It is recommended by the General Conference to the Traveling Preachers, to advise our friends in general to purchase a lot of ground in each circuit, and to build a Preacher's house thereon, and to furnish it with, at least, heavy furniture, and to settle the same on trustees appointed by the Quarterly Conference, according to the Deed of Settlement published in our form of Discipline.

2. The General Conference recommend to all the circuits, in cases where they are not able to comply with the above request, to rent a house for the married Preacher

the receipt of the Conference thereon, shall be sent to the Book Agents, and be placed to the credit of the person who paid the same.

23. Any Traveling Preacher who may publish any work or book of his own, shall be responsible to his Conference for any obnoxious matter or doctrine therein contained.

24. No Editor, Agent, or Clerk employed in the Book Concern, or in any department belonging to it, shall be allowed in any case to publish or sell books as his own private property, or employ his time for other parties.

PART V.

TEMPORAL ECONOMY.

CHAPTER I.

RAISING SUPPLIES—CHURCH BUILDINGS, ETC.

SECTION I.

Methods for raising Annual Supplies for the Propagation of the Gospel, and making up the Allowance of Preachers.

1. The more effectually to raise the amount necessary to meet the above-mentioned allowances of the effective Ministers and Preachers, let there be made weekly class collections in all our societies where it is practicable; and in such circuits and stations where the stewards approve, large classes may be divided into two or three financial classes, to consist of not more than twelve members and a collector appointed by the preacher, (by and with the advice and consent of the stewards,) whose duty

it shall be to collect weekly, monthly, or quarterly, as the case may be determined, from each member of the class what they agree to pay, and the money when collected shall be paid regularly to the class-leader, to be brought up by him to the leaders' meeting or Quarterly Conference, as the case may be.

2. To provide to meet the claims that may be presented and determined at the Annual Conference, every Preacher shall make an annual collection in every congregation of his charge, and the money so collected shall be lodged in the hands of the steward or stewards and brought or sent to the ensuing Annual Conference.

3. Let the annual produce of the Charter Fund, as divided among the several Annual Conferences, be applied with the above contributions, but so as not to militate against the rules of the Charter Fund, and also the annual dividend arising from the profits of the Book Concern. Out of the money so collected and brought to the respective Annual Conferences, let the various allowances agreed upon in accordance with the provisions of part ii, chap. i, § 4; chap. iii, § 3; chap. iv, § 2, be made up.

4. Effective men who have not been able

to obtain their allowance from the people where they have labored may present a claim to the Conference, to be paid out of the money at the disposal of the Conference, and such claim may be paid, or any part thereof, as the Conference may determine.

SECTION II.

Building and Renting Houses for the Use of Traveling Preachers.

Quest. What advice or direction shall be given concerning the building or renting of dwelling-houses for the use of the married Traveling Preachers?

Answ. 1. It is recommended by the General Conference to the Traveling Preachers, to advise our friends in general to purchase a lot of ground in each circuit, and to build a Preacher's house thereon, and to furnish it with, at least, heavy furniture, and to settle the same on trustees appointed by the Quarterly Conference, according to the Deed of Settlement published in our form of Discipline.

2. The General Conference recommend to all the circuits, in cases where they are not able to comply with the above request, to rent a house for the married Preacher

and his family, (when such are stationed upon their circuits respectively,) and that the Annual Conferences do assist to make up the rents of such houses as far as they can, when the circuit cannot do it.

The Stewards of each circuit and station shall be a standing committee (where no trustees are constituted for that purpose) to provide houses for the families of our married Preachers, or to assist the Preachers to obtain houses for themselves when they are appointed to labor among them.

3. It shall be the duty of the Presiding Elders and Preachers to use their influence to carry the above rules respecting building and renting houses for the accommodation of Preachers and their families into effect. In order to this, each Quarterly Conference shall appoint a committee, (unless other measures have been adopted,) who, with the advice and aid of the Preachers and Presiding Elders, shall devise such means as may seem fit to raise moneys for that purpose. And it is recommended to the Annual Conferences to make a special inquiry of their members respecting this part of their duty.

4. Any preacher who shall refuse to occupy the house which may be provided for

him by the Stewards, shall thereby forfeit his claim on the Stewards to the amount of said house rent. *Nevertheless*, this rule shall not apply to those preachers whose families are either established within the bounds of their circuits, or are so situated that, in the judgment of the Stewards, or the above-mentioned committee, it is not necessary, for the benefit of the circuit, to remove them.

SECTION III.

Building Churches, and the Order to be observed therein.

Quest. 1. Is anything advisable in regard to building churches?

Answ. 1. Let all our churches be built plain and decent, and with free seats wherever practicable; but not more expensive than is absolutely unavoidable, otherwise the necessity of raising money will make rich men necessary to us. But if so, we must be dependent on them, yea, and governed by them. And then farewell to Methodist discipline, if not doctrine too.

2. In order more effectually to prevent our people from contracting debts which they are not able to discharge, it shall be

the duty of the Quarterly Conference of every circuit and station where it is contemplated to build a house or houses of worship, to secure the ground or lot on which such house or houses are to be built, according to our deed of settlement, which deed must be legally executed; and also said Quarterly Conference shall appoint a judicious committee of at least three members of our Church, who shall form an estimate of the amount necessary to build; and three fourths of the money, according to such estimate, shall be secured or subscribed before any such building shall be commenced.

In all cases where debts for building houses of worship have been, or may be, incurred contrary to, or in disregard of, the above recommendation, our members and friends are requested to discountenance, by declining pecuniary aid to all agents who shall travel abroad beyond their own circuits or districts for the collection of funds for the discharge of such debts: except in such peculiar cases as may be approved by an Annual Conference, or such agents as may be appointed by their authority.

3. In future we will admit no charter, deed, or conveyance for any house of wor-

ship to be used by us, unless it be provided in such charter, deed, or conveyance, that the trustees of said house shall at all times permit such ministers and preachers belonging to the Methodist Episcopal Church as shall from time to time be duly authorized by the General Conference of the ministers of our Church, or by the Annual Conferences, to preach and expound God's holy word, and to execute the discipline of the Church, and to administer the sacraments therein, according to the true meaning and purport of our deed of settlement.

SECTION IV.

Trustees, and their Duties and Responsibilities.

1. Let nine trustees be appointed for holding Church property, where proper persons can be procured; otherwise seven or five.

2. When a new board of trustees is to be created, it shall be done (except in those States and Territories where the statutes provide differently) by the appointment of the Preacher in charge, or the Presiding Elder of the district.

3. When any one or more of the trustees

shall die, or cease to be a member or members of the said Church according to the rules of the Discipline as aforesaid, then and in such case it shall be the duty of the stationed Minister or Preacher (authorized as aforesaid) who shall have the pastoral charge of the members of the said Church, (except in those States and Territories where the statutes provide differently,) to call a meeting of the remaining trustees as soon as conveniently may be: and when so met, the said Minister or Preacher shall proceed to nominate one or more persons to fill the place or places of him or them whose office [or offices] has [or have] been vacated as aforesaid. *Provided*, the person or persons so nominated shall have been one year a member or members of the said Church immediately preceding such nomination, and be at least twenty-one years of age; and the said trustees, so assembled, shall proceed to elect, and by a majority of votes appoint, the person or persons so nominated to fill such vacancy or vacancies, in order to keep up the number of nine trustees forever; and in case of an equal number of votes for and against the said nomination, the stationed Minister or Preacher shall have the casting vote.

Provided, nevertheless, That if the said trustees, or any of them, or their successors, have advanced, or shall advance, any sum or sums of money, or are or shall be responsible for any sum or sums of money, on account of the said premises, and they, the said trustees, or their successors, be obliged to pay the said sums of money, they, or a majority of them, shall be authorized to raise the said sum or sums of money by a mortgage on the said premises, or by selling the said premises, after notice given to the Pastor or Preacher who has the oversight of the congregation attending divine service on the said premises, if the money due be not paid to the said trustees, or their successors, within one year after such notice given; and if such sale take place, the said trustees, or their successors, after paying the debt and other expenses which are due from the money arising from such sale, shall deposit the remainder of the money produced by the said sale in the hands of the Steward or Stewards of the society belonging to or attending divine service on said premises; which surplus of the produce of such sale, so deposited in the hands of the said Steward or Stewards, shall be at the disposal of the Quarterly Conference; which said Quarterly Conference shall dispose of the said money, according to the best of their judgment, for the use of the said society.

4. No person shall be eligible as a trustee to any of our houses, churches, or schools, who is not a regular member of our Church.

5. No person who is a trustee shall be ejected while he is in joint security for money, unless such relief be given him as is demanded, or the creditor will accept.

6. The Board of Trustees of every circuit or station shall be responsible to the Quarterly Conference of said circuit or station, and shall be required to present a report of its acts during the preceding year.

SECTION V.

*A Form of a Deed of Settlement.**

Quest. What shall be done for the security of our preaching-houses, and the premises belonging thereto?

Answ. Let the following plan of a deed of settlement be brought into effect in all

* For the old and full form of this deed, see Appendix, section 1.

possible cases, and as far as the laws of the States respectively will admit of it. But each Annual Conference is authorized to make such modification in the deeds as they may find the different usages and customs of law require in the different States and Territories, so as to secure the premises firmly by deed, and permanently to the Methodist Episcopal Church, according to the true intent and meaning of the following form of a deed of settlement: anything in the said form to the contrary notwithstanding.

THIS INDENTURE, made this day of in the year of our Lord one thousand hundred and between of the in the State of (if the grantor be married, insert the name of his wife) of the one part, and trustees, in trust for the use and purposes hereinafter mentioned, all of the in the State of aforesaid, of the other part, WITNESSETH, that the said (if married, insert the name of his wife,) for and in consideration of the sum of specie, to in hand paid, at and upon the sealing and delivery of these presents, the receipt whereof is hereby acknowledged, hath (or have) given, granted, bargained, sold, released, confirmed, and conveyed, and by these presents doth (or do) give, grant, bargain, sell, release, confirm, and convey unto them the said and their successors, (trustees, in trust for the uses and purposes hereinafter mentioned and declared,) all the estate, right, title, interest, property, claim, and demand whatsoever, either in law or equity, which he, the said (if married, here insert the name of his wife) hath (or have) in, to, or upon all and singular a certain lot, or piece of land, situate, lying, and being in the and State aforesaid, bounded and butted as follows, to-wit, (here insert the several courses and distances of the land to the place of beginning,) containing and laid out for acres of land, together with all and singular the houses, woods, waters, ways, privileges, and appurtenances thereto belonging, or in anywise pertaining: TO HAVE AND TO HOLD all and singular, the above-mentioned and described lot or piece of land, situate, lying, and being as aforesaid, together with all and singular the houses, woods, waters, ways, and privileges thereto belonging, or in anywise appertaining unto them the said and their successors in office forever, in trust, that they shall erect and build, or cause to be erected and built thereon, a house or place of worship for the use of the members of the Methodist Episcopal Church in the United States of America, according to the rules and discipline which from time to time may be agreed upon, and adopted by the ministers and preachers of the said Church at their General Conferences in the United States of America; and in further trust and confidence that they shall at all times, forever hereafter, permit such ministers and preachers belonging to the said Church as shall from time to time be duly authorized by the General Conference of the ministers and preachers of the said Methodist Episcopal Church, or by the Annual Conferences authorized by the said General Conference, to preach and expound God's holy word therein; And the said doth by these presents warrant, and forever defend, all and singular the before-mentioned and described lot or piece of land, with the appurtenances thereto belonging, unto them the said and their successors, chosen and appointed as aforesaid, from the claim or claims of him the said his heirs and assigns, and from the claim or claims of all persons whatever. In testimony whereof, the said (if married, insert the name of his wife) have hereto set their hands and seals, the day and year aforesaid.

Sealed and delivered in the presence of us, (Two witnesses.)

Grantor's (L. S.)
His wife's (L. S.)

Received the day of the date of the above-written indenture, the consideration therein mentioned in full.

Witness.] Grantor's (L. S.)

County, *ss.*

BE IT REMEMBERED, that on the day of in the year of our Lord one thousand personally appeared before me, one of the justices of the peace in and for the County of and State of the within named the grantor, (if married, insert the name of his wife,) who acknowledge the within deed of trust to be their act and deed, for the uses and purposes therein mentioned and declared; and she, the said wife of the said being separate and apart from her said husband by me examined, declared that she had made the same acknowledgment freely and with her own consent, without being induced thereto through fear or threats of her said husband. In testimony whereof I have hereto set my hand and seal, the day and year first above written.

Here the justice's name. (L. S.)

CHAPTER II.

BOUNDARIES.

SECTION I.

The Boundaries of the Annual Conferences.

1. BALTIMORE CONFERENCE shall be composed of the Baltimore, Washington, Potomac, Winchester, Rockingham, Roanoke, and Lewisburgh Districts, as they existed at the adjournment of 1857, the line through the city of Baltimore being the following, namely: Leaving the line of the Patapsco River and Jones's Falls at Monument-street, and along that street to Eutaw-street, down Eutaw-street to Ross-street; thence along Ross-street to Dolphin-street; thence along Dolphin-street to Grundy-street; out Grundy-street to the City line, and along the line of the City Corporation to Jones's Falls; Emory and Whatcoat Stations being exceptions, and belonging to East Baltimore Conference.

2. BLACK RIVER CONFERENCE shall include, together with Rose Circuit, that part of the State of New York, west of Troy Conference, not embraced in the East Genesee Conference, as far south as the

Erie Canal, and all the Societies on the immediate banks of the Canal, except Utica, Canastota, Montezuma, and Port Byron.

3. CALIFORNIA CONFERENCE shall embrace the State of California and the Sandwich Islands, together with the Territory of Utah, and so much of New Mexico as lies west of the Rocky Mountains, until these may be formed into a Mission Conference.

4. CENTRAL ILLINOIS CONFERENCE shall embrace all that part of the State of Illinois north of the Illinois Conference, and south of the following line, namely: Beginning on the Mississippi River at Meredocia, down said Meredocia to its mouth; thence easterly to Center School House, so as to embrace Center Society in Central Illinois Conference; thence to the mouth of Mud Creek on Green River, up said river to the mouth of Coal Creek; thence up said creek to the Rock Island and Chicago Railroad; thence with said railroad to La Salle; thence with Illinois River to the mouth of Kankakee River; thence with said river to the Indiana State Line, so as to embrace La Salle Station.

5. CENTRAL OHIO CONFERENCE shall be bounded by a line commencing at the

northwest corner of the State of Ohio; thence east by the north line of the State to a point north of the mouth of Sandusky River; thence south to the mouth of Sandusky River, excluding Port Clinton Circuit; thence up said river to Upper Sandusky, excluding Tiffin City, and including Fremont and Upper Sandusky; thence along the Pittsburgh, Fort Wayne, and Chicago Railroad to Crestline, including Bucyrus Station and Crestline; thence along the Cleveland, Columbus, and Cincinnati Railroad, by the curve to Delaware, leaving Cardington and Galion in Central Ohio Conference, and so much of the town of Delaware, as lies on the east side of the Olentangy River, in North Ohio Conference; thence along the said Railroad to the north line of the Ohio Conference; thence west along the north line of the Ohio and Cincinnati Conferences to the west line of the State; thence north along the west line of the State to the place of beginning.

6. CINCINNATI CONFERENCE shall commence at the mouth of Ohio Brush Creek, and shall be bounded on the south by the Ohio River, and on the west by the Indiana State Line, to the southern bounds of the Central Ohio Conference, at the southwest

corner of Dark County; thence eastwardly along said line, so as to exclude the Sidney and Delaware Districts of the Central Ohio Conference, to the boundary of the Ohio Conference at its junction with the southern line of the Central Ohio Conference; thence in a southeasterly direction with said western line of the Ohio Conference to the place of beginning.

7. DETROIT CONFERENCE shall include all that part of the State of Michigan lying east of the principal meridian line, the upper peninsula, and those parts of Minnesota and Wisconsin adjacent to Lake Superior.

8. EAST BALTIMORE CONFERENCE shall embrace the territory belonging to the Baltimore Conference previous to its division in 1857, not included in the present bounds of the Baltimore Conference, excepting Asbury and Orchard-street Station, and Baltimore City Mission and Finchburgh Church, which shall belong to the Baltimore Conference.

9. EAST GENESEE CONFERENCE shall contain all that part of the State of New York west of the Black River, Oneida, and Wyoming Conferences, and east of Genesee River, including the whole of the City of Rochester, together with so much of the

State of Pennsylvania as is included in the Troy and Hornellsville Districts, and including Laporte Circuit.

10. EAST MAINE CONFERENCE shall include that part of the State of Maine not included in the Maine Conference.

11. ERIE CONFERENCE shall be bounded on the north by Lake Erie; on the east by a line commencing at the mouth of Cattaraugus Creek; thence up said creek to the village of Gowanda, leaving said village in the Genesee Conference; thence to the Alleghany River at the mouth of Tunungwant Creek; thence up said creek southward to the ridge dividing between the waters of Clarion and Sinnemahoning Creeks; thence southward to the head of Mahoning Creek; thence down said creek, exclusive of the Milton Society, but including Putneyville in the Bethlehem Circuit, to the Alleghany River; thence across said river in a northwesterly direction to the Western Reserve Line, including the north part of Butler and Newcastle Circuits, and also including Petersburgh; thence west to the Ohio Canal; thence along said canal to Lake Erie, including Akron and all of Cleveland lying east of the Cuyahoga River.

12. GENESEE CONFERENCE shall include all that part of the State of New York west of the East Genesee Conference, including Lima, except so much as is included in the Erie Conference, and also so much of the State of Pennsylvania as is embraced in the Olean District.

13. GERMAN CONFERENCE.—There shall be an Annual Conference in Germany, to be denominated the *German Mission Annual Conference*, embracing also the missions in France and Switzerland where the German language is spoken, which Conference shall possess all the rights, powers, and privileges of other Annual Conferences, excepting that of sending delegates to the General Conference, and of drawing its annual dividend from the avails of the Book Concern and the Chartered Fund, and of voting on constitutional changes proposed in the Discipline.

14. ILLINOIS CONFERENCE shall include that part of Illinois not included in the Southern Illinois Conference, south of the following line, namely: Beginning at Warsaw on the Mississippi River; thence to Vermont; thence to the mouth of Spoon River; thence up the Illinois River to the northwest corner of Mason County; thence to the junction of the Central and the

Alton and Chicago Railroads, leaving Mackinaw Circuit in the Central Illinois Conference; thence to the southwest corner of Iroquois County; thence east to the Indiana State line, leaving the Western Charge in Bloomington in the Central Illinois Conference, and including State Line City in Illinois Conference.

15. INDIANA CONFERENCE shall be bounded as follows, namely: Beginning at the mouth of Silver Creek on the Ohio River, thence with said Creek to the Jeffersonville Railroad; thence by said railroad to Rockford; thence by the east fork of White River to Columbus; thence by the Madison and Indianapolis Railroad to Franklin; thence by the plank Road to the bluffs of White River; thence north by said river to the Donation line of Indianapolis; thence east by said line to Meridian-street; thence north by said street to its intersection with Market-street; thence west by Market-street to the Donation line; thence south by said Donation line to the National Road; thence by the National Road west to the Greencastle State Road, one and a half miles west of Stilesville; thence with the said State Road to the town plat of Greencastle; thence due south

to Seminary-street, including the Second Charge in Greencastle, together with lot No. 153; thence due south to the southern border of the College grounds, upon a line equally dividing the College Campus and building; thence due west to the Walnut fork of Eel River; thence down said river to its intersection with the National Road; thence with said road to the western line of the state, including all the towns on the National Road west of Indianapolis, in the Indiana Conference, except Terre Haute; thence by the State line to the mouth of the Wabash River; thence by the State line to the mouth of Silver Creek, the place of beginning.

16. IOWA CONFERENCE shall be bounded as follows, namely: Commencing at Davenport on the Mississippi River, and running down said river to the south line of the state of Iowa; thence on that line west to the southwest corner of Apanoose County; thence north to the Des Moines River, and up said river to the south line of Boone County; thence east to the Iowa River, and down said river to Iowa City; thence eastward on the line of railway to the place of beginning, leaving Davenport and Iowa City in the Upper Iowa Conference,

and the intermediate towns upon the line in the Iowa Conference.

17. KANSAS CONFERENCE shall embrace the State or Territory of Kansas, and the State of Texas, and that portion of New Mexico east of the Rocky Mountains.

18. KENTUCKY CONFERENCE shall include the State of Kentucky, excepting so much of said State as is included in the Western Virginia Conference.

19. LIBERIA CONFERENCE.—There shall be an Annual Conference on the Western Coast of Africa, to be denominated the *Liberia Mission Annual Conference*, possessing all the rights, powers, and privileges of other Annual Conferences, except that of sending delegates to the General Conference, and of drawing its annual dividend from the avails of the Book Concern and of the Chartered Fund, and of voting on constitutional changes proposed in the Discipline.

20. MAINE CONFERENCE shall include that part of the State of Maine lying west of the Kennebeck River, from its mouth to the Great Bend below Skowhegan, and of a line running from thence north to the State line, (including Skowhegan and Augusta Stations in Maine Conference,) and

that part of New Hampshire lying east of the White Hills and north of the waters of the Ossipee Lake, and the town of Gorham.

21. Michigan Conference shall include all that part of the State of Michigan lying west of the principal meridian line; and the Indian Missions, in the lower peninsula, shall be connected with the Michigan Conference.

22. Minnesota Conference shall include the State of Minnesota, except so much as is included in the Detroit Conference.

23. Missouri and Arkansas Conference shall include the States of Missouri and Arkansas.

24. Nebraska Conference shall embrace the Territory of Nebraska.

25. Newark Conference shall include all that part of the State of New Jersey not included in the New Jersey Conference; Staten Island, and so much of the States of New York and Pennsylvania as is now included in the Paterson and Newton Districts.

26. New England Conference shall include all the State of Massachusetts, lying east of the Green Mountains, not embraced in the New Hampshire and Providence Conferences.

27. NEW HAMPSHIRE CONFERENCE shall include all the State of New Hampshire not embraced in the Maine Conference, and that part of the State of Massachusetts northeast of the Merrimac River.

28. NEW JERSEY CONFERENCE shall include that part of the State of New Jersey lying south of the following line, namely: Beginning with Raritan Bay, and running up said bay and river to New Brunswick; thence along the turnpike road in a direct line to Lambertville on the Delaware, including the city of New Brunswick and Lambertville Station.

29. NEW YORK CONFERENCE shall consist of the territory now included in the New York, Poughkeepsie, Newburgh, Prattsville, Monticello, and Rhinebeck Districts.

30. NEW YORK EAST CONFERENCE shall consist of the New York East, the Bridgeport, New Haven, and Long Island Districts, including in the city of New York all those charges lying east of a line running through the Third Avenue, Bowery, Chatham-street, and Broadway.

31. NORTH INDIANA CONFERENCE shall include all of Northeastern Indiana bounded north by Michigan, east by Ohio, includ-

ing Union City; south by the National Road, and west by the Michigan Road as far north as South Bend; thence down St. Joseph River to the Michigan State line; also the town of Logansport, all towns on the National Road east of Indianapolis, and so much of the city of Indianapolis within the Donation as lies north of Market-street and east of Meridian-street.

32. NORTH OHIO CONFERENCE shall be bounded on the north by the north line of the State of Ohio, east by the Erie and Pittsburgh Conferences, on the south by the Ohio Conference, and on the West by the Central Ohio Conference.

33. NORTHWEST INDIANA CONFERENCE shall embrace all of Northwest Indiana, bounded north by the State and Lake of Michigan; east by the Michigan Road and St. Joseph River; south by Indiana Conference, and west by the State of Illinois; also the city of Terre Haute, with so much of the city of Indianapolis within the Donation as lies north of Market-street and west of Meridian-street, with all towns on the Michigan Road except Logansport.

34. NORTHWEST WISCONSIN CONFERENCE shall be bounded as follows, namely: Beginning on the Mississippi River on the

north line of town twelve; thence east to the east line of range one, east; thence north to the north line of town forty; thence west to the St. Croix River; thence down the St. Croix and Mississippi Rivers to the place of beginning.

35. OHIO CONFERENCE shall commence at the southeast corner of the North Ohio Conference, and thence south, following the course of the Muskingum River to its junction with the Ohio River, including the city of Zanesville and the town of Marietta; thence down the Ohio River to the mouth of Ohio Brush Creek; thence north to the southeast corner of Fayette county, leaving Sinking Spring Circuit west of said line, and Bethesda and Rapid Forge Societies, with Staunton and Bloomingsburgh Circuits, east of said line, except Fairfield, which shall be left west of said line; thence northwest to the western boundary of said county of Fayette; thence in a due north direction to the southern boundary of Central Ohio Conference, leaving Vienna Circuit west of said line; thence east with southern line of Central Ohio Conference in part, and of the North Ohio Conference to the place of beginning, leaving so much of the Marysville Circuit, including Marys-

ville, as lies north of the Springfield, Mount Vernon, and Pittsburgh Railroad, in the Central Ohio Conference, and retaining Milford in the Ohio Conference; and thence along the south line of the Central Ohio Conference, including St. Paul's Charge, in Delaware, and Stratford Circuit in the Ohio Conference, leaving, however, the Ohio Wesleyan University within the bounds of the Central Ohio Conference.

36. ONEIDA CONFERENCE shall include that part of the State of New York south of the Black River Conference and east of Cayuga Lake, and north of a line running east from Newfield to Ithaca; from thence following the Catskill turnpike to Greene, and from thence following the same line of road through Masonville to the New York Conference, including all the Charges on said line, excepting Lisle and Whitney's Point Charge; from thence on the south west line of the Troy Conference to the Erie Canal.

37. OREGON CONFERENCE shall embrace the State of Oregon and Washington Territory.

38. PHILADELPHIA CONFERENCE shall include the Eastern shore of Maryland and Virginia, the State of Delaware, and all

that part of Pennsylvania lying between the Susquehanna and Delaware Rivers, except so much as is in East Baltimore, Wyoming, and Newark Conferences, including Naglesville in Philadelphia Conference.

39. PITTSBURGH CONFERENCE shall be bounded on the north by the Erie Conference; on the east by a line running along the top of the Alleghany Mountains to the southern line of the State of Pennsylvania; thence west along the line of the Western Virginia Conference to the Ohio River; thence down said river to the mouth of the Muskingum River; thence up said river, exclusive of the towns Marietta and Zanesville, to the Tuscarawas River; thence up said river, including the town of Massillon, to the line of the Erie Conference.

40. PROVIDENCE CONFERENCE shall include that part of the State of Connecticut lying east of Connecticut River, all the State of Rhode Island, with Millville and Blackstone in Massachusetts, and also that part. of the State of Massachusetts lying southeast of a line drawn from the northeast corner of the State of Rhode Island to the north of the Neponset River, which line shall so run as to leave Walpole Sta-

tion, Foxborough, and Quincy Point with in the bounds of the New England Conference.

41. ROCK RIVER CONFERENCE shall embrace all the north part of the State of Illinois, north of the Central Illinois Conference, so as to include the city of Peru.

42. SOUTHEASTERN INDIANA CONFERENCE shall include all of Southeastern Indiana bounded north by the National Road, east by Ohio, south by the Ohio River, and west by the Indiana Conference; with so much of the city of Indianapolis within the Donation as lies south of Market-street and east of Meridian-street; and all the towns and societies on the line between Indiana and Southeastern Indiana Conferences.

43. SOUTHERN ILLINOIS CONFERENCE shall include all that part of the State of Illinois south of the following line, namely: Beginning at Gilead on the Mississippi River in Calhoun County, thence to the northwest corner of Jersey County, including Kane and Woodbury; thence to Honey Point; thence to Hillsborough, leaving Hillsborough Station in the Illinois Conference; thence east through Fayette and Effingham Counties to the northeast corner of Jasper County; thence with the north

line of Jasper and Crawford Counties to the Wabash River.

44. TROY CONFERENCE shall include the Troy, Albany, (including Richmondville and Fort Plain Stations,) Saratoga, Poultney, and Plattsburgh Districts.

45. UPPER IOWA CONFERENCE shall embrace all that part of the State of Iowa not embraced in the Iowa and Western Iowa Conferences.

46. VERMONT CONFERENCE shall include the State of Vermont, exclusive of the appointments embraced in the Troy and Poultney Districts, except Mount Holly and Cuttingsville, which shall be included in the Vermont Conference.

47. WESTERN IOWA CONFERENCE shall be bounded as follows, namely: Commencing on the Missouri River at the southwest corner of the State of Iowa, and running up said river to the north line of Harrison County; thence east to the western line of the Iowa Conference; thence with said line to the south line of the State; thence west on said line to the place of beginning.

48. WESTERN VIRGINIA CONFERENCE shall be bounded as follows: Beginning at the southwest corner of the Pennsylvania line, thence along said line to the northeast

corner of Ohio County, Virginia, so as to include Wheeling Creek Mission and Triadelphia Circuits; thence the most direct way to Short Creek, so as to include the Short Creek and Liberty Circuits; thence down said Creek to the Ohio River; thence down said river to the mouth of Little Sandy River; thence up said river, so as to include all that part of Kentucky lying east of said river in the Guyandotte District: On the south and east it shall be bounded by the Baltimore Conference to the Pennsylvania State line: thence westward by said line to the place of beginning.

49. West Wisconsin Conference shall include all the southwestern portion of the State of Wisconsin not included in the Wisconsin and Northwest Wisconsin Conferences.

50. Wisconsin Conference shall be bounded on the north by the Upper Peninsula of Michigan, on the east by Lake Michigan, on the south by Illinois State line, and on the west by a line beginning at the southeast corner of Green County, and running north on the Range line between range nine (9) and ten (10) east, to the north line of town twenty (20;) thence west on said line to the east line of Range

one; thence north on said line to Lake Superior.

51. WYOMING CONFERENCE shall include the southern part of the State of New York not included in the Oneida, East Genesee, and New York Conferences, including Lisle and Whitney's Point Charge; together with that part of Pennsylvania bounded on the west by the East Genesee, south by the [East] Baltimore, Philadelphia, and Newark Conferences, and east by the Newark and New York Conferences.

SECTION II.

The Arrangement of the German Work.

1. The German work in California shall remain as it now is, in connection with the California Conference.

2. The Quincy and Beardstown Districts, as they now are, (except Marshall mission,) including Pekin station and Peoria mission, from Chicago German District, in the Rock River Conference, shall be connected with the Illinois Conference.

3. All the German work in Kansas and Nebraska Territories, with the western part of the State of Iowa, and all the German work in the State of Missouri west of

the Osage River, shall be connected with the Kansas Conference.

4. All the German work in the State of Minnesota, and all the territory in the western part of the State of Wisconsin that lies west of a straight line due north, commencing in the south on the eastern edge of Badax county, (including said county,) and running due north to Lake Superior, shall be connected with the Minnesota Conference.

5. The German missions in the east shall remain in connection with the New York Conference.

6. The North Ohio and Michigan German Districts, including Defiance circuit, in the State of Ohio, shall remain in connection with the North Ohio Conference.

7. All the German work in the eastern and central parts of the State of Iowa, with Rock Island and Freeport missions, Galena station, in the State of Illinois, and all the missions which are now included in the Galena District, in the State of Wisconsin, shall be connected with the Upper Iowa Conference.

8. The Chicago and Wisconsin German Districts as they now are, except Pekin station and Peoria mission, in the State of

Illinois, shall be connected with the Rock River Conference.

9. The German work now connected with the Southeast Indiana Conference, including Marshall mission, in the State of Illinois, except Defiance circuit, in the State of Ohio, and Lower Wabash, shall remain connected with the aforesaid Conference.

10. The German work now connected with the Southern Illinois Conference, including Lower Wabash mission, in the State of Illinois, shall remain in connection with that Conference.

11. The German work in the Cincinnati Conference shall remain connected with that Conference for the present.

PART V·I.

CHAPTER I.

OF SLAVERY.

Quest. What shall be done for the extirpation of the evil of slavery?

Answ. We declare that we are as much as ever convinced of the great evil of Slavery. We believe that the buying, selling, or holding of human beings, to be used as chattels, is contrary to the laws of God and nature, and inconsistent with the Golden Rule and with that Rule in our Discipline which requires all who desire to continue among us to "do no harm," and to "avoid evil of every kind." We therefore affectionately admonish all our Preachers and People to keep themselves pure from this great evil, and to seek its extirpation by all lawful and Christian means.

INDEX.

APPENDIX.

1. Form of a Deed of Settlement for Church Property.

Quest. What shall be done for the security of our preaching-houses, and the premises belonging thereto?

Answ. Let the following plan of a deed of settlement be brought into effect in all possible cases, and as far as the laws of the states respectively will admit of it. But each annual conference is authorized to make such modification in the deeds as they may find the different usages and customs of law require in the different states and territories, so as to secure the premises firmly by deed, and permanently to the Methodist Episcopal Church, according to the true intent and meaning of the following form of a deed of settlement; anything in the said form to the contrary notwithstanding.

This Indenture, made this day of in the year of our Lord one thousand hundred and between of the in the state of (if the grantor be married, insert the name of his wife) of the one part, and trustees, in trust for the uses and purposes hereinafter mentioned, all of the in the state of aforesaid, of the other part, Witnesseth, that the said (if married, insert the name of his wife) for and in consideration of the sum of specie to in hand paid, at and upon the sealing and delivery of these presents, the receipt whereof is hereby acknowledged, hath (or have) given, granted, bargained, sold, released, confirmed, and conveyed, and by these presents doth (or do) give, grant, bargain, sell, release, confirm, and convey unto them, the said and their successors, (trustees in trust for the uses and purposes hereinafter mentioned and declared,) all the estate, right, title, interest, property, claim, and demand whatsoever, either in law or equity, which he the said (if married, here insert the name of his wife) hath (or have) in, to, or upon all and singular a certain lot, or piece of land, situate, lying, and being in the and state aforesaid, bounded and butted as follows, to wit, (here insert the several courses and distances of the land to the place of beginning,) containing and laid out for acres of land, together with all and singular the houses, woods, waters, ways, privileges, and appurtenances thereto belonging, or in any wise pertaining: TO HAVE AND TO HOLD all and singular the above-mentioned and described lot or piece of land, situate, lying, and being as aforesaid, together with all and singular the houses, woods, waters, ways, and privileges thereto belonging, or in any wise appertaining unto them the said and their successors in office for ever in trust, that they shall erect and build, or cause to be erected and built thereon, a house or place of worship for the use of the members of the Methodist Episcopal Church in the United States of America, according to the rules and discipline which from time to time may be agreed upon and adopted by the ministers and preachers of the said Church at their General Conferences in the United States of America; and in further trust and confidence that they shall at all times, for ever hereafter, permit such ministers and preachers belonging to the said Church, as shall from time to time be duly authorized by the General Conferences of the ministers and preachers of the said Methodist Episcopal Church, or by the annual conferences authorized by the said General Conference, to preach and expound God's holy word therein; and in further trust and confidence, that as often as any one or more of the trustees herein before mentioned shall die, or cease to be a member or members of the said Church according to the rules and discipline as aforesaid, then and in such case it shall be the duty of the stationed minister or preacher (authorized as aforesaid) who shall have the pastoral charge of the members of the said Church, to call a meeting of the remaining trustees as soon as conveniently may be: and when so met, the said minister or preacher shall proceed to nominate one or more persons to fill the place or places of him or them whose office or offices has (or have) been vacated as aforesaid. *Provided*, the person or persons so nominated shall have been one year a member or members of the said Church immediately preceding such nomination, and be at least twenty one years of age; and the said trustees, so assembled, shall proceed to elect, and by a majority of votes appoint, the person or persons so nominated to fill such vacancy or vacancies, in order to keep up the number of nine trustees for ever; and in case of an equal number of votes for and against the said nomination, the stationed minister or preacher shall have the casting vote.

Provided nevertheless, That if the said trustees, or any of them, or their successors, have advanced, or shall advance, any sum or sums of money, or are or shall be responsible for any sum or sums of money on account of the said premises, and they, the said trustees or their successors, be obliged to pay the said sums of money, they, or a majority of them, shall be authorized to raise the said sum or sums of money, by a mortgage on the said premises, or by selling the said premises, after notice given to the pastor or preacher who has the oversight of the congregation attending divine service on the said premises, if the money due be not paid to the said trustees, or their successors, within one year after such notice given; and if such sale take place, the said trustees, or their successors, after paying the debt and other expenses which are due from the money arising from such sale, shall deposit the remainder of the money produced by the said sale in the hands of the steward or stewards of the society belonging to or attending divine service on said premises; which surplus of the produce of such sale, so deposited in the hands of said steward or stewards, shall be at the disposal of the next annual conference authorized as aforesaid; which said annual conference shall dispose of the said money, according to the best of their judgment, for the use of the said society. And the said doth by these presents warrant, and for ever defend, all and singular the before-mentioned and described lot or piece of land, with the appurtenances thereto belonging unto them the said and their successors, chosen and appointed as aforesaid, from the claim or claims of him the said his heirs and assigns, and from the claim or claims of all persons whatever. In testimony whereof, the said (if married, insert the name of his wife) have hereto set their hands and seals, the day and year aforesaid.

Sealed and delivered in the presence of us (Two witnesses.)

Grantor's (L. S.)
his wife's (L. S.)

Received the day of the date of the above-written indenture, the consideration therein mentioned in full.
Witness.]

Grantor's (L. S.)

County, ss.

BE IT REMEMBERED, that on the day of in the year of our Lord one thousand personally appeared before me, one of the justices of the peace, in and for the county of and state of the within-named the grantor (if married, insert the name of his wife) acknowledged the within deed of trust to be their act and deed for the uses and purposes therein mentioned and declared; and she the said wife of the said being separate and apart from her said husband, by me examined, declared that she had made the same acknowledgment, freely and with her own consent, without being induced thereto through fear or threats of her said husband. In testimony whereof I have hereto set my hand and seal, the day and year first above written.

Here the justice's name. (L. S.)

II. ORDERS AND RESOLUTIONS OF THE GENERAL CONFERENCE.

Complaints against Bishops.

Whereas it appears that individuals sometimes forward to the General Conference complaints against the administration of the Bishops without due notice being given them; and

Whereas we consider that our superintendents should be apprised of these proceedings beforehand in writing; therefore,

Resolved, That, in the judgment of this General Conference, it is improper for such complaints to be made without due notice being furnished to the Bishops in writing.—*Journal*, 1860, p. 231.

Whereas, under the rule which says, "A Bishop shall decide all questions of law in an annual conference subject to an appeal to the General Conference," a custom has grown up of evoking episcopal decisions touching the administration of the Discipline outside of the annual conferences; and

Whereas the opinions of the Bishops, given in writing in the intervals of the annual conferences, are sometimes regarded as decisions of law, binding in the administration of Discipline; and

Whereas these decisions and opinions are sometimes in conflict with each other, springing up from questions growing out of peculiar and ever varying circumstances; and

Whereas it is the judgment of this Conference that the use made of the rule aforesaid was not intended by the General Conference which established it, that General Conference intending it for the administration of the conferences, and not of the individual pastors; therefore,

1. *Resolved*, That every administrator of the Discipline is responsible to the proper authorities for his administration of the rules of the Church, and may not plead episcopal decisions as law.

2. *Resolved*, That while the counsels of our superintendents are to be highly respected, and to be considered of great value in the administration of Discipline, their decisions are not to be regarded as having the force of *law* outside of the annual conferences.—*Journal*, p. 428.

The Rights of Transferred Preachers.

When a Preacher is transferred from one Conference to another, his rights, privileges, and responsibilities in the Conference to which he is transferred shall date from the date of his transfer, unless it be especially provided otherwise by the Bishop by whom the transfer is made.

But it will not be lawful for him to vote twice on the same Constitutional Question, or be counted twice in the same year as the basis of the Election of Delegates to the General Conference, nor vote for delegates to the General Conference in any Conference where he is not counted as a part of the basis of representation.—*Appendix*, *Journal*, 1860, p. 364.

A Preacher may not be appointed to the same Charge when divided.

It is a violation of a rule of Discipline for a Bishop to continue a Preacher in a station or circuit for more than two years, notwithstanding the station may be divided into two or more stations or circuits.—*Journal*, 1836, p. 473.

Chairman not to charge Committees.

Resolved, That it is the judgment of this General Conference that in all trials of preachers, whether by Committee or before a Conference, and in all appeals, it is improper for the Presiding Elder or Chairman of the Committee, or other party presiding at the trial, to deliver after the pleadings a charge to the Committee explaining the evidence and setting forth the merits of the case.—*Appendix*, *Journal*, 1860, p. 363.

The Right of a President to Adjourn a Conference —To refuse to put a Motion, etc.

The President of an Annual or a Quarterly Meeting Conference has the right to adjourn the Conference over which he presides when in his judgment all the business prescribed by the Discipline to such Conference shall have been transacted; *provided*, that, if an exception be taken by the Conference to his so adjourning it, the exception shall be entered upon the Journals of such Conference.—*Journal*, 1840, p. 121.

When a Bishop presiding in an Annual Conference decides a question of law by request of the Conference, if a motion is made which would reverse the decision of the Bishop under the plea that the Conference has the right to apply the law in the case, should the motion be put, and the Conference be allowed to set aside the law under the pretense of applying it?

Answer. No. When a question of law has been decided by a Bishop in an Annual Conference, that decision cannot be reversed or set aside except by the action of the ensuing General Conference, to which body an appeal may be taken by the Annual Conference or by any member thereof.—*Journal*, 1860, p. 297.

If a motion is made in an Annual or Quarterly Conference, which, if passed, would be a positive violation of Discipline, should the President put the motion and allow the Discipline to be set aside, or what should he do?

Answer. He should refuse to put the motion. —*Journal*, 1860, p. 297.

The President of an Annual or a Quarterly Meeting Conference has the right to decline putting the question on a motion, resolution, or report when, in his judgment, such motion, resolution, or report does not relate to the proper business of a Conference; *provided*, that in all such cases the President, on being required by the Conference to do so, shall have inserted in the Journals of the Conference his refusal to put the question on such motion, resolution, or report, with his reason for so refusing; *and provided*, that when an Annual Conference shall differ from the President on a question of law, they shall have a right to record their dissent on the Journals, provided there shall be no discussion on the subject.—*Journal*, 1840, p. 121.

Conferences in all Cases of Appeal to send forward the Documents, etc.

Resolved, That the Liberia Annual Conference, as well as every other Conference, is directed, in all cases of the condemnation or censure of any of its members, to send forward to the General Conference the minutes and documents of the trial.—*Journal*, 1860, p. 203.

A tie Vote on an Appeal does not Change the Action of the Court below.

In any ecclesiastical Court of Appeals, when the three questions, Shall the decision of the lower Court be affirmed? Shall the case be remanded for a new trial? Shall the former decision be reversed? have been successively put, and there is a tie vote on each, then in what condition does it leave the appellant?

Resolved, That it is the sense of this Conference that when the motions to affirm, to remand, and to reverse have been successively put and lost, the decision of the Court below stands as the final adjudication of the case.—*Journal*, 1860, p. 248.

Rights of Quarterly Conferences in a certain Case.

Question. In case a Quarterly Conference recommend the renewal of the license of an exhorter, is the presiding elder under obligation to renew the license?

Answer. He is.—*Journal*, 1860, pp. 228, 229.

Presiding Elder's Duty in relation to the General Missionary Committee.

Resolved, That the Presiding Elders in the Annual Conferences be requested to furnish to the member of the General Missionary Committee, appointed to represent the Mission Districts within which they labor, a written statement of the condition of the Missions within their bounds, and their pecuniary wants, prior to the annual meeting of the Committee.—*Journal*, 1860, p. 295.

[See article "General Missionary Committee" in Appendix B.]—ED.

Receiving or Expelling Members Improperly—Its Influence on the Relations of Parties, etc.

If a preacher in charge of any work receive a person into the Church contrary to the Discipline, can the Annual Conference correct the administration, and declare that the person, having been received contrary to Discipline, is therefore not a member?

Answer. No. This question was decided by the General Conference of 1852 by the adoption of the following resolution:

Resolved, That when an Annual Conference decides that a preacher having charge has received or expelled a member contrary to the Discipline, the decision does not exclude the member so received, but restores the member so expelled. (General Conference Journal, page 73.)—*Journal*, 1860, p. 297.

When a member is expelled from the Church, and complaint is made against the administrator to his Annual Conference for maladministration, and the Conference decide that the person was expelled contrary to Discipline, what is the relation of the member expelled from the Church? Does the act of the Annual Conference restore the character of the member, so that the charges on which he was expelled are so annulled that the preacher may legally give him a letter before said charges are disposed of by trial or withdrawn?

Answer. The act of the Annual Conference does not restore his character, but simply his membership, and when so restored he is placed in the position which he occupied before he was tried; that is, he is an accused member, and hence the preacher is not at liberty to give him a certificate of membership. — *Journal*, 1860, p. 298.

Irregularity in the reception of a Member is not a bar to Trial.

May a person who has not been formally received into full connection in the Church, but has for a term of years enjoyed all the privileges of a member, and is supposed by the preacher in charge and society to be a member, plead the fact of his nonreception as a bar to proceedings in case of alleged immorality?

Answer. No.—*Journal*, 1860, p. 298.

The Right to take Testimony before a Committee, etc.

Testimony taken before a committee sitting in the case of an accused member of an Annual

Conference, is to be received as evidence on the trial of said minister before the Annual Conference.—*Journal*, 1848, p. 126.

A Preacher who withdraws from the Conference under Charges cannot Appeal from the Record.

When a member of an Annual Conference gives notice to the Conference that he has withdrawn from the Church or Conference, and at the same time there be *charges* ready to be presented against him, and he has knowledge of such *charges* previous to his notice of withdrawal, and he has been marked upon the Journal of the Annual Conference as withdrawn under *charges*, has such member a right to appeal to the General Conference from such record of the Annual Conference?

Answer. He has not.—*Journal*, 1860, p. 298.

A Preacher who refuses to attend his Work.

Can a traveling preacher, during the interval of the Annual Conference of which he is a member, be suspended for refusing to attend to the work assigned him?

Answer. It is the duty of a Presiding Elder "to take charge of all the Elders and Deacons in his District," and to "take care that every part of our Discipline be enforced." Now our Discipline provides that no Elder or Deacon "who ceases to travel without the consent of the Annual Conference, certified under the hand of the President of the Conference, except in cases of sickness, debility, or other unavoidable circumstances, shall on any account exercise the peculiar functions of his office, or even be allowed to preach among us." Hence, any Elder or Deacon who refuses to go to the work assigned him ("except in cases of sickness," etc.) may be suspended "in the interval of the Annual Conference;" but the "*final* determination in all such cases is with" the Conference.—*Journal*, 1860, p. 297.

Right to Try a Member in the Interval of the Annual Conference, etc.

An Annual Conference has a right, when charges are preferred against one of their number, and the case cannot be tried during their session for want of testimony, to refer it to the Presiding Elder who may have charge of him, under the rule for the trial of immoral ministers in the interval of an Annual Conference.—*Journal*, 1848, p. 128.

Amenability for Maladministration.

To whom is a preacher amenable on a complaint of maladministration?

Answer. To the Annual Conference of which he is a member.—*Journal*, 1860, p. 301.

Maladministration not to try a Member who wishes to remove, but is under imputation.

When a member wishes to remove his residence out of any particular charge, and there are, in the judgment of the preacher in charge, sufficient reasons for withholding a certificate, and the member is willing to be tried, he shall be held guilty of maladministration unless he proceed in the trial of such person.—*Journal*, 1848, p. 98.

When a member receives a certificate of membership from a preacher having charge of a Circuit or Station, he is responsible for his moral conduct (from the date of his certificate until he joins) to the Society receiving him upon that certificate.—*Journal*, 1848, p. 126.

Removal of Church Membership and Certificates, etc.

No preacher is under obligation to give a certificate of membership to any member of the Methodist Episcopal Church unless said member wishes to remove his membership to another charge in the Methodist Episcopal Church, though, as a matter of courtesy, he may give a recommendation to a member in good standing who wishes to unite with another evangelical denomination.—*Journal*, 1848 p. 59.

The Right of a Quarterly Conference to remand for a New Trial, etc.

When an appeal is taken by an expelled member to the Quarterly Conference, and the Conference remand the case back for a new trial, what is the precise relation of the appellant? Is he an accused member, and must the preacher proceed to try him again, or is he restored to his membership in good standing?

Answer. He is an accused member, and the preacher should proceed to try him again unless the charges are withdrawn.—*Journal*, 1860, p. 298.

Is there in the Discipline anything authorizing a Quarterly Meeting Conference to remand a case for a new trial?

Answer. When the preacher in charge differs "in judgment from the majority of the Society, or the select number, concerning the guilt or innocence of the accused person," and refers the case to the Quarterly Conference, that body has "authority to order a new trial." (Discipline, p. 130.) And in other cases, the power to remand for what the Conference may deem sufficient cause, is inherent in that body as an appellate court.—*Journal*, 1860, p. 301.

New Testimony not Admissible.

In no case of an appeal can new evidence be admitted.—*Journal*, 1860, p. 137.

The right of Appeal may be forfeited.

When an expelled member has, by neglect or otherwise, forfeited his *right* of appeal, may a subsequent Quarterly Conference, if it desire to do so, grant him the *privilege* of an appeal?

Answer. No.—*Journal*, 1860, p. 298.

Probationers not a Right to bring Charges.

Question. Has a probationer in our Church the right to prefer charges against a member of our Church?

Answer. He has not.—*Journal*, 1860, p. 228.

None but Members of the Church have a Right to Petition.

Resolved, That it is the sense of this Conference that under the call for memorials, etc., no member has a right to present petitions from any except members of our own Church.—*Journal*, 1860, p. 180.

Whereas, during the pendency of the Chapter on Slavery, the following amendment was offered as explanatory of the chapter, "Provided that this section is understood to be only advisory,"

Resolved, That said amendment was rejected by this body because we regard the chapter in itself so clearly declarative and advisory as not to require any such explanation.—*Journal*, 1860, p. 261.

American Bible Society.

This General Conference cherishes the most cordial and undiminished confidence in the American Bible Society, and hereby recommends the ministers and members of the Methodist Episcopal Church to co-operate with it, and exert themselves to carry out its noble and benevolent designs.

In view of the importance of this whole subject, we hereby recommend to each minister in the connection to preach at least once a year on this subject, and generally at the time when he makes his annual collection for the Bible cause.—*Journal*, 1856, pp. 85, 86.

Order on Lay Delegation.

1. *Resolved*, That we, the Delegates of the Annual Conferences of the Methodist Episcopal Church in General Conference assembled, hereby approve of the introduction of Lay Representation into this body when it shall be ascertained that the Church desires it.

2. *Resolved*, That all our preachers in charge, stationed within the United States and Territories, be and they are hereby required to lay the subject of Lay Representation in the General Conference before the male members over twenty-one years of age, and in full connection in their several charges, at a meeting duly notified on two successive Sabbaths, said meet-

ings to be held at some convenient period between the sessions of the respective Annual Conferences in 1861 and 1862, and the results to be certified to the Annual Conference next succeeding the taking of the vote by the preacher in charge, specifying the number voting for and the number voting against Lay Representation, and be entered upon the Journals; and that each Annual Conference shall, through its Secretary, furnish to the presiding Bishop a certified copy of the result. The form and manner of presenting the vote to the male members of the Church shall be by ballot, and as follows: "For Lay Representation," or, "Against Lay Representation."

3. *Resolved*, That the Bishops be, and are hereby instructed to lay the same question and in the same form before the Annual Conferences at their sessions in 1862; and that each Annual Conference, through its Secretary, shall furnish the presiding Bishop with a certified copy of the result.

4. *Resolved*, That the Bishops be requested to report the results of these several votes to the General Conference at its next session.—*Journal*, 1860, p. 290.

A.—CONFERENCE JOURNALS.

[The editor has judged it might be useful to insert, from the Journal of the General Conference, the following extract in relation to the duties of the Secretaries of Annual Conferences.]

Most of the journals that have been examined are well kept, some of them in superior style; we wish we could say this of every journal. But some give evidence of inattention to several important parts of a full journal, such as neglecting, 1st. To page their journals. 2d. To furnish marginal references. 3d. To record resolutions passed by the Conference. 4th. Noticing the adoption of important reports without saying they were filed. All resolutions passed by the Conference should be spread upon the journal. It is the opinion of the Committee that important papers referred to on the Journal as filed should be brought with the Journals to the General Conference. Secretaries of Annual Conferences cannot be too careful in journalizing the matters pertaining to the trial of a member of the Annual Conference, correctly marking and referring to all papers used as testimony in such cases, so that, in case of an appeal, the journal and papers will present a fair and full showing of the case as passed upon by the Conference.—*Journal*, 1860, p. 225.

B.—GENERAL MISSIONARY COMMITTEE, 1860–4.

I. DISTRICT.—New England, Providence, New York East, Troy, Vermont, New Hampshire, Maine, and East Maine Conferences,

FREDERIC UPHAM, Providence Conference.

II. DISTRICT.—New York, Newark, New Jersey, Philadelphia, East Baltimore, Baltimore, Western Virginia, Pittsburgh, California, and Oregon Conferences,

WILLIAM COOPER, Philadelphia Conference.

III. DISTRICT.—Oneida, Black River, Wyoming, East Genesee, Genesee, Erie, North Ohio, and Central Ohio Conferences,

MOSES HILL, Erie Conference.

IV. DISTRICT.—Ohio, Cincinnati, Kentucky, Southeastern Indiana, Indiana, Northwestern Indiana, North Indiana, Michigan, and Detroit Conferences,

FERNANDO C. HOLLIDAY, S. E. Indiana Conf.

V. DISTRICT.—Rock River, Central Illinois, Upper Iowa, Minnesota, Northwestern Wisconsin, West Wisconsin and Wisconsin Conferences,

W. G. MILLER, Wisconsin Conference.

VI. DISTRICT.—Illinois, Southern Illinois, Missouri and Arkansas, Iowa, Western Iowa, Kansas, and Nebraska Conferences,

JOHN H. POWER, Iowa Conference.

C.—BOOK COMMITTEE AT NEW YORK.

New York and New York East Conferences,
MORRIS D'C. CRAWFORD.

Providence, New England, Maine, East Maine, and New Hampshire Conferences,
WILLIAM H. PILLSBURY.

Philadelphia, New Jersey, and Newark Conferences,
SAMUEL Y. MONROE.

Baltimore and East Baltimore Conferences,
CHARLES B. TIPPETT.

Vermont, Troy, and Black River Conferences,
GARDNER BAKER.

Oneida, East Genesee, Genesee, and Wyoming Conferences,
GEORGE PECK.

Erie, Pittsburgh, and Western Virginia Conferences,
JOHN COIL.

D.—BOOK COMMITTEE AT CINCINNATI.

Ohio Conference,
JOSEPH M. TRIMBLE.

Cincinnati Conference,
JOHN T. MITCHELL.

Central Ohio and North Ohio Conferences,
ELNATHAN C. GAVITT.

Indiana and Southeastern Indiana Conferences,
JOHN KIGER.

North Indiana and Northwestern Indiana Conferences,
O. V. LEMON.

Detroit and Michigan Conferences,
W. E. BIGELOW.

Illinois and Southern Illinois Conferences,
PETER CARTWRIGHT.

Rock River and Central Illinois Conferences,
RICHARD HANEY.

Iowa and Upper Iowa Conferences,
THOMAS E. CORKHILL.

Wisconsin, West Wisconsin, and Minnesota Conferences,
BENJAMIN F. CRARY.

Missouri, Arkansas, Kansas, and Nebraska Conferences,
SAMUEL HUFFMAN.

Journal, 1860, p. 291.

COURSE OF STUDY.

I. For Candidates for Admission on Trial in the Traveling Connection.

English Grammar — Modern Geography — True's Logic—Newman's Rhetoric.

[Read Porter's Compendium of Methodism —Wesley's Sermons.]

II. For Conference Membership and for Orders.

FIRST YEAR. — The Bible — Doctrines.

The Existence of God—The Attributes of God, namely: Unity, Spirituality, Eternity, Omnipotence, Ubiquity, Omniscience, Immutability, Wisdom, Truth, Justice, Mercy, Love, Goodness, Holiness — The Trinity in Unity — The Deity of Christ — The Humanity of Christ — The Union of Deity and Humanity — Personality and Deity of the Holy Ghost — Depravity — Atonement — Repentance — Justification by Faith — Regeneration — Adoption — The Witness of the Spirit — Growth in Grace — Christian Perfection — Possibility of Final Apostasy — Immortality of the Soul — Resurrection of the Body — General Judgment — Rewards and Punishments.

[The examination on the above to be strictly Biblical, requiring the candidate to give the statement of the doctrine and the Scripture proofs. To prepare for this he should read the Bible by course, and make a memorandum of the texts upon each of these topics as he proceeds.]

Watson's Institutes, 1st Part — Wesley's Plain Account of Christian Perfection — Fletcher's Appeal — Clark's Mental Discipline.

Essay or Sermon.

[Read Wesley's Notes — Stevens's History of Methodism — Willson's General History]

[SECOND YEAR. — The Bible — Sacraments.

The Sacrament of Baptism: Its Nature, Design, Obligation, Subjects, and Mode — The Sacrament of the Lord's Supper: Its Nature, Design, and Obligation.

[Mode of study and examination same as on Bible in the first year.]

Watson's Institutes, 2d Part — Peck's Christian Perfection, 12mo. — Fletcher's Christian Perfection — Strickland's Manual of Biblical Literature — Methodist Discipline — Mitchell's Ancient Geography.

Essay or Sermon.

[Read Bishop Emory's Defense of our Fathers — Powell on Apostolical Succession — Dr. Emory's History of the Discipline — Wesley on Original Sin, and Wesley's Doctrinal Tracts — Johnston's Natural Philosophy.]

THIRD YEAR.— Bible — History and Chronology.

Watson's Institutes, 3d Part — Butler's Analogy — Peck's Rule of Faith — Hibbard on Baptism — Ruter's Church History — Blair's Lectures on Rhetoric, University Edition — Hedge's Logic.

Essay or Sermon.

[Read Bangs's History of the Methodist Episcopal Church — Elliott on Romanism — Fletcher's Works — Rollin's Ancient History — Smith's Patriarchal Age — Hallam's Middle Ages — Russell's Modern Europe.]

FOURTH YEAR.—Review of the whole Course.

Watson's Institutes, 4th Part — Claude's Essay on the Composition and Delivery of a Sermon — Horne's Introduction, abridged — Stewart's Mental Philosophy.

Essay or Sermon.

[Read Smith's Hebrew People — Mosheim's Ecclesiastical History — Townley's Illustrations of Biblical Literature — Watson's Sermons — History of the United States — Stevens's Church Polity — Hibbard's Palestine: Its Geography and Bible History.]

III. For Local Preachers who are Candidates for Deacon's Orders.

The Bible — Doctrines.

The Existence of God — The Attributes of God, namely: Unity, Spirituality, Eternity, Omnipotence, Ubiquity, Omniscience, Immutability, Wisdom, Truth, Justice, Mercy, Love, Goodness, Holiness — The Trinity in Unity — The Deity of Christ — The Humanity of Christ — The Union of Deity and Humanity — Personality and Deity of the Holy Ghost — Depravity — Atonement — Repentance — Justification by Faith — Regeneration — Adoption — The Witness of the Spirit — Growth in Grace — Christian Perfection — Possibility of Final Apostasy — Immortality of the Soul — Resurrection of the Body — General Judgment — Rewards and Punishments.

The Bible — Sacraments.

The Sacrament of Baptism: Its Nature, Design, Obligation, Subjects, and Mode — The Sacrament of the Lord's Supper: Its Nature, Design, and Obligation.

[The examination on the above subjects is to be strictly Biblical, requiring the candidates to give the statement of the doctrine and the Scripture proofs. To prepare for this, he should read the Bible by course, and make a memorandum of the texts upon each of these topics as he proceeds.]

Systematic Divinity.

Watson's Institutes, Part First and Second — Wesley's Plain Account of Christian Perfection — Fletcher's Appeal.

Church Government: Methodist Discipline.

Common English: English Grammar — Modern Geography.

[Read Watson's Life of Wesley — Wesley's Sermons — Emory's Defense of our Fathers — Powell on Apostolical Succession.]

IV. FOR LOCAL PREACHERS WHO ARE CANDIDATES FOR ELDER'S ORDERS.

Review of the previous course.

Bible — History.

The leading events recorded in the Old and New Testaments.

Systematic Divinity: Watson's Institutes, Part Third and Fourth.

An Essay or Sermon.

[Read Fletcher's Checks — Smith's Hebrew People — Ruter's Church History — Porter's Compendium of Methodism.]

V. FOR THE GERMAN TRAVELING PREACHERS.

FIRST YEAR. — The Bible — Doctrines.

(Same as in the English Course.)

Wesley's Sermons, vol. i — Compendium of Methodism — Church History, published by the Norddeutschen Verein, vol. i — Wurst's Grammar of the German Language, sections 1–8, 43–80 — A Written Sermon.

[Read Watson's Apology for the Bible — D'Aubigné's History of the Reformation, vol. i — Fletcher's Appeal.]

N.B.—Those who find Wurst's Grammar too difficult may use Splittegarb's Grammar. To those who understand the English language we recommend Woodbury's Grammar of the German Language.

SECOND YEAR.—The Bible — Sacraments.

(Same as in the English Course.)

Hare on Justification — Wesley's Christian Perfection — The Discipline — Church History, vols. ii and iii — Wurst's Grammar of the German Language, sections 9–42 — A Written Sermon on Baptism.

[Read Nelson's Causes of Infidelity — Haldane's Genuineness and Justification of the Holy Scriptures — D'Aubigné's History of the Reformation, vol. ii — Wesley and his Coadjutors, by W. Nast.]

THIRD YEAR.

Kurtz's Sacred History — The Philosophy of the Plan of Salvation — Zeller's Psychology — Church History, vols. iv and v — Woodbury's Grammar of the English Language — A Written Sermon on the Difference of Justification and Sanctification.

[Read D'Aubigné's History of the Reformation, vol. iii — Ralston's Elements of Divinity — Hibbard on Baptism.]

FOURTH YEAR.

Lisco's Exposition of the Apostles' Creed — Nast's General Introduction into the New Testament — Bishop Baker's Guide to the Discipline — Church History, vols. vi and vii — Woodbury's Grammar of the English Language — A Written Sermon on the Lord's Supper.

[Read Weber's Universal History — D'Aubigné's History of the Reformation, vols. iv and v — Stevens's History of Methodism, vol. i.]

VI. FOR GERMAN LOCAL DEACONS.

Compendium of Theology, by L. S. Jacoby — Discipline — Wesley's Sermons, vol. i — Hare on Justification.

[Read Fletcher's Appeal — Compendium of Methodism — Watson's Apology.]

VII. FOR GERMAN LOCAL ELDERS.

Lisco's Exposition of the Apostles' Creed — Wesley's Sermons, vol. ii — Wesley's Christian Perfection — Calwer Church History.

[Read Nast's Wesley and his Coadjutors — Haldane on the Genuineness and Inspiration of the Holy Scriptures — Zeller's Psychology.]

PUBLISHED BY CARLTON & PORTER,

200 Mulberry-street, N. Y.

INFANT CHURCH MEMBERSHIP;

Or, the Spiritual and Permanent Character of the Abrahamic Covenant. By Rev. SAMUEL GREGG. Edited by Rev. D. W. CLARK, D.D. 16mo.

This book discusses in a clear and able manner the right of children of believing parents to membership in the Christian Church.

THE LORD'S SUPPER.

By Rev. SAMUEL LUCKEY, D.D. With an Introduction, by Rev. BISHOP JANES. 18mo.

ECONOMY OF METHODISM.

Economy of Methodism, Illustrated and Defended. In a Series of Papers. By Rev. THOMAS BOND, D.D. 8vo.

A most admirable exposition.

PLEASANT PATHWAYS;

Or, Persuasives to Early Piety: containing Explanations and Illustrations of the Beauty, Safety, and Pleasantness of a Religious Life: being an Earnest Attempt to persuade Young People of both sexes to Seek Happiness in the Love and Service of Jesus Christ. By DANIEL WISE. Large 16mo.

AN ESSAY ON SECRET PRAYER,

As the Duty and Privilege of Christians. By JOSEPH ENTWISLE. 18mo.

PUBLISHED BY CARLTON & PORTER,

200 Mulberry-street, N. Y.

LIFE OF JACOB GRUBER.

An interesting biography of one of the most remarkable preachers of his day. By W. P. STRICKLAND. 12mo.

It is a rare book, full of wit and wisdom. It contains his memorable sermon for which he was indicted by the grand jury of Frederic county, Maryland, and charged with inciting an insurrection among the slaves.

It also contains a full account of the trial, and the defense of Roger B. Taney, the present Chief Justice of the Supreme Court of the United States. A finely engraved portrait by Ritchie is in the volume. Send on your orders.

THE HOMILIST:

A series of Sermons for Preachers and Laymen, original and selected. By ERWIN HOUSE, A. M. 12mo.

The Homilist, just issued, is a compilation of sermons, and sketches of sermons, selected from the vast reservoir of such kind of literature published in England under the same title. It is said to embrace the very best contained in the numerous volumes from which it is compiled, as well as a number of original discourses. We hope that it will find favor, and prove a blessing to many.

BISHOP WAUGH.

A Discourse commemorative of Rev. Beverly Waugh, D. D., late Senior Bishop of the Methodist Episcopal Church. Delivered before the General Conference in Buffalo, May 11, 1860, by Rev. THOMAS A. MORRIS, D. D., present Senior Bishop of the Methodist Episcopal Church. Published by order of the General Conference. 12mo.

PUBLISHED BY CARLTON & PORTER,
200 Mulberry-street, N. Y.

EARLY METHODISM

Within the Bounds of the old Genesee Conference, from 1788 to 1828; or, the First Forty Years of Wesleyan Evangelism in Northern Pennsylvania, Central and Western New York, and Canada; containing Sketches of interesting Localities, exciting Scenes, and prominent Actors. By George Peck, D.D. 12mo.

THE GREAT REFORMATION.

History of the Great Reformation in England, Ireland, Scotland, Germany, France, and Italy. By Rev. Thomas Carter. 12mo.

This is a book which must be interesting to every class of readers. It is fresh from the pen of an American writer, and written from an American standpoint.

LIGHT IN THE VALLEY;

Or, the Life and Letters of Mrs. Hannah Bocking. By Miss M. Annesley. 18mo.

THE STORY OF A POCKET BIBLE.

A Book for all Classes of Readers. Ten illustrations. Wide 16mo.

THE CHRISTIAN LAWYER:

Being a Portraiture of the Life and Character of William George Baker. 12mo.

This is a well-written memoir, and deserves to be generally read. A good holiday gift-book for our legal friends.

PUBLISHED BY CARLTON & PORTER,

200 Mulberry-street, N. Y.

ESSAY ON CHURCH POLITY.

Comprising an Outline of the Controversy on Ecclesiastical Government, and a Vindication of the Ecclesiastical System of the Methodist Episcopal Church. By A. STEVENS, LL.D. 18mo.

CLAUDE'S ESSAY

On the Composition of a Sermon. By Rev. JOHN CLAUDE. Edited by Rev. CHARLES SIMEON, M. A., Senior Fellow of King's College, Cambridge. 18mo.

THEODICY;

Or, Vindication of the Divine Glory, as Manifested in the Constitution and Government of the Moral World. By ALBERT TAYLOR BLEDSOE, Professor of Mathematics in the University of Mississippi. 8vo.

INTRODUCTION.—Of the Possibility of a Theodicy. PART I.—The Existence of Moral Evil, or Sin, consistent with the Holiness of God. PART II.—The Existence of Natural Evil, or Suffering, consistent with the Goodness of God. CONCLUSION.—A Summary View of the Principles and Advantages of the foregoing System.

BRIDAL GREETINGS,

With Marriage Certificate. By Rev. D. WISE. 24mo.

PROMOTION OF REVIVALS.

Helps to the Promotion of Revivals. By Rev. J. V. WATSON, D.D. 12mo.

PUBLISHED BY CARLTON & PORTER,

200 Mulberry-street, N. Y.

BAKER ON THE DISCIPLINE.

A Guide-Book in the Administration of the Discipline of the Methodist Episcopal Church. By Bishop Baker. Revised edition. 12mo.

A valuable book for all our preachers in relation to the usages of the Church in matters of administration.

CLASS-LEADERS' MANUAL;

Or, an Essay on the Duties, Difficulties, Qualifications, Motives, and Encouragements of Class-Leaders. To which is prefixed an Introductory Chapter on the History and Scriptural Basis of Class-Meetings. By Rev. Charles C. Keys, of the New York Annual Conference. 18mo.

CLASS-MEETINGS.

Treatise on Class-Meetings. By Rev. John Miley, A. M. With an Introduction by Rev. Thomas A. Morris, D. D., one of the Bishops of the Methodist Episcopal Church.

COLES'S CONCORDANCE.

A New Concordance of the Holy Scriptures of the Old and New Testaments. By Rev. George Coles. 24mo.

CHURCH POLITY.

A Discourse on Methodist Church Polity. By T. A. Morris, D. D., Senior Bishop of the Methodist Episcopal Church. 18mo.

PUBLISHED BY CARLTON & PORTER.

200 Mulberry-street, N. Y.

COMPENDIUM OF METHODISM.

A Compendium of Methodism: embracing the History and Present Condition of its various Branches in all Countries; with a Defense of its Doctrinal, Governmental, and Prudential Peculiarities. By Rev. JAMES PORTER, D.D. Revised edition. 12mo.

This is a most valuable and reliable manual of the Church, presenting in a lucid and interesting light whatever is peculiar to Methodism in its doctrines, government, institutions, and usages. This book should be in the hands of every Methodist.

HISTORY OF DISCIPLINE.

History of the Discipline of the Methodist Episcopal Church. By Rev. ROBERT EMORY. Revised and brought down to 1856, by W. P. STRICKLAND, D.D. 12mo.

DOCTRINAL TRACTS.

A Collection of Interesting Tracts, explaining several Important Points of Scripture Doctrine. By Rev. J. WESLEY, A.M. Published by Order of the General Conference. 18mo.

HIBBARD ON THE PSALMS.

The Psalms Chronologically Arranged, with Historical Introductions, and a General Introduction to the whole Book. By F. G. HIBBARD. 8vo.

LIFE OF HENRY LONGDEN,

Minister of the Gospel. Compiled from his Letters, Diary, etc. 18mo.

PUBLISHED BY CARLTON & PORTER,
200 Mulberry-street, N. Y.

SKETCH BOOK;

Or, Miscellaneous Anecdotes, illustrating a variety of Topics proper to the Pulpit and the Platform. By WILLIAM C. SMITH, of the New York Conference. Wide 16mo.

INSIDE VIEWS OF METHODISM.

Or, a Hand-Book for Inquirers and Beginners. By WILLIAM REDDY, of the Oneida Annual Conference. 18mo.

THE HEAVENLY CONQUEROR;

Or, the Great Combat between Christ and Satan for the Human Soul. By Rev. WILLIAM MORLEY PUNSHON, Wesleyan Minister. 12mo.

MISSIONARY AMONG CANNIBALS;

Or, the Life of John Hunt, who was eminently successful in Converting the People of Fiji from Cannibalism to Christianity. By GEORGE STRINGER ROWE. 12mo.

LIFE AND TIMES OF ASBURY.

The Pioneer Bishop; or, the Life and Times of Francis Asbury. By W. P. STRICKLAND. With an Introduction by NATHAN BANGS, D.D. 12mo.

THE PIONEERS OF THE WEST;

Or, Life in the Woods. By W. P. STRICKLAND. 12mo.

NEW BOOKS

PUBLISHED BY CARLTON & PORTER,

200 Mulberry-street, N. Y.

PRONOUNCING BIBLE.

Large 8vo.

We have lately issued the best Bible in print, A PRONOUNCING BIBLE, having these advantages: 1. The proper names are divided and accented, so that a child can pronounce them correctly. 2. Each book has a short introduction, showing just what every reader ought to know about it. 3. It has a much improved class of references. 4. It contains a map of Old Canaan and its surroundings, and one of Palestine, according to the latest discoveries.

WHEDON'S COMMENTARY.

A Commentary on the Gospels of Matthew and Mark. Intended for Popular Use. By D. D. WHEDON, D. D. 12mo.

The first volume of this long-promised work is now ready. It is a 12mo. of 422 closely printed pages, embracing a fine map of Palestine and other valuable illustrations. If it shall fail to meet with general favor we shall be greatly disappointed. Tens of thousands of copies should be put in immediate circulation. THE CHEAPEST *book for the price that we have issued in many months.*

JOURNAL OF THE GENERAL CONFERENCE

of the Methodist Episcopal Church, held in Buffalo, N. Y., 1860. Edited by Rev. WILLIAM L. HARRIS, D. D., Secretary of the Conference. 8vo.

AUTOBIOGRAPHY OF DAN YOUNG,

A New England Preacher of the Olden Time. Edited by W. P. STRICKLAND. 12mo.

Methodist Book Concern,

200 MULBERRY-STREET.

CARLTON & PORTER,

PUBLISHERS OF

BIBLES, COMMENTARIES, SINGING BOOKS, HYMN BOOKS, DICTIONARIES, BIOGRAPHIES, GIFT-BOOKS, ETC.,

Making some four hundred volumes, besides a great variety of other works in the departments of Biblical Literature, Experimental and Practical Religion, etc., etc. Also about twelve hundred bound volumes of

SABBATH-SCHOOL LIBRARY BOOKS,

THE LARGEST LIST PRINTED IN THIS COUNTRY.

Besides multitudes of Question Books, Hymn Books, Picture Books, Catechisms, Cards, and Tracts, adapted to children of all ranks and ages. They are ordered and prized by schools of all denominations. Then we have a large list of other works, beautifully illustrated for gift-books for children and youth, which are equal to any in the land.

NEW BOOKS.

HISTORY OF METHODISM,

IMMORTALITY OF THE SOUL......
LIFE OF ADAM CLARKE, D.D., LL.D.
THE POET PREACHER.............
PALISSY THE POTTER.............
PRONOUNCING BIBLE.............
MOTHER'S MISSION.................
MY SISTER MARGARET ....
LIFE OF ASBURY ....
INSIDE VIEWS OF METHODISM ...
PLEASANT PATHWAYS ....
THE LORD'S SUPPER ....
THE MINISTRY OF LIFE...........

PUBLISHED BY CARLTON & PORTER,

200 Mulberry-street, N. Y.

NEW ENGLAND DIVINES.

Sketches of New England Divines. By Rev. D. SHERMAN. 12mo.

Giving true and interesting biographical sketches of the following distinguished divines: John Cotton, Richard Mather, Roger Williams, Increase Mather, Cotton Mather, Eleazer Mather, John Warham, Jesse Lee, Jonathan Edwards, Elijah Hedding, Timothy Dwight, Wilbur Fisk, Ezra Stiles, Lemuel Haynes, Billy Hibbard, Timothy Merritt, Jonathan D. Bridge, Nathaniel Emmons, Joshua Crowell, George Pickering, Stephen Olin.

LIFE OF DR. ADAM CLARKE.

By Rev. J. W. ETHERIDGE, M.A. With a Portrait. 12mo.

THE IMMORTALITY OF THE SOUL

And the Final Condition of the Wicked carefully considered. By Rev. ROBERT W. LANDIS. 12mo.

PETER CARTWRIGHT.

Autobiography of Peter Cartwright. Edited By W. P. STRICKLAND. 12mo.

This is one of the most interesting autobiographies of the age. It is having a most rapid and extensive sale.

CHART OF LIFE.

By Rev. JAMES PORTER, D. D. 12mo.

The design of this book is to indicate the dangers and securities connected with the voyage of life, all which are accurately and admirably described.

www.ingramcontent.com/pod-product-compliance
Lightning Source LLC
LaVergne TN
LVHW020222110826
845151LV00003B/800

* 9 7 8 1 4 2 5 5 3 2 4 7 5 *